Cakes
bakes & biscuits

First published in the United Kingdom in 2016 by
National Trust Books
1 Gower Street
London
WC1E 6HD

An imprint of Pavilion Books Company Ltd

ISBN 9781909881853
A CIP catalogue record for this book is available from the British Library.

20 19 18 17 16
10 9 8 7 6 5 4 3 2 1

Reproduction by Mission Productions Ltd, Hong Kong
Printed and bound by Toppan Leefung Printing Ltd, China

This book can be ordered direct from the publisher at
www.pavilionbooks.com

Cakes

bakes & biscuits

National Trust

Contents

Introduction

The great British teatime is a time-honoured tradition, and who doesn't enjoy the prospect of settling down with a fragrant cup of freshly brewed tea accompanied by the finest of homemade cakes? Here you will find recipes for over a hundred mouthwatering bakes; from classic cakes to bite-sized treats and superb scones to tantalising teabreads. Try your hand at regional classics such as Bara Brith, Bath Buns or Banbury Cakes, or go one step further and make your own delicious fruit jams to go with any of the tempting scone recipes.

Whether you are a seasoned baker looking for inspiration or trying your hand in the kitchen for the first time, there are delicious bakes to suit every taste. Discover the straightforward golden rules for successful baking, choose a handful of delicious recipes and you'll be well on your way to creating a teatime worthy of the Queen herself.

The
Basics

Classic Cake Recipes

Madeira cake
17.5cm (7in) round cake

225g (8oz) plain flour
1 teaspoon baking powder
175g (6oz) butter, softened
175g (6oz) caster sugar
Grated zest of ½ unwaxed lemon
3 large free-range eggs
2 tablespoons milk

1 Preheat the oven to 180°C, 350°F, gas mark 4. Grease and line an 18cm (7in) round cake tin.

2 Mix together the flour and baking powder in a large bowl. Beat together the butter, sugar and lemon zest until light and fluffy. Beat in the eggs, one at a time, adding 2 tablespoons of flour with the last two. Fold in the remaining flour, then mix in the milk.

3 Turn into the prepared tin and bake for 1 hour or until a skewer inserted into the centre comes out clean.

4 Remove from the oven and turn out onto a wire rack to cool.

Lemon drizzle cake
450g (1lb) loaf

50g (2oz) butter, softened
75g (3oz) self-raising flour
75g (3oz) caster sugar
1 large free-range egg
2 tablespoons milk
Grated zest and juice of 1 unwaxed lemon
50g (2oz) granulated sugar

1 Preheat the oven to 160°C, 325°F, gas mark 3. Grease and line a 450g (1lb) loaf tin.

2 Put the butter, flour, caster sugar, egg, milk and lemon zest into a large bowl or freestanding mixer and beat until the batter is very pale and fluffy.

3 Spoon the batter into the prepared tin and smooth the surface. Bake for about 30 minutes, or until the cake is firm and springy to the touch, and a knife or skewer comes out clean.

4 Mix the lemon juice and granulated sugar in a bowl and as soon as the cake comes out of the oven, spread this mixture over the surface. Leave the cake to cool in the tin to soak up the tangy lemon topping. Turn it out of the tin when it is completely cold.

> Try using other flavours with the lemon drizzle recipe: any citrus fruit works well.

Whisked sponge cake
20cm (8in) cake

3 large free-range eggs, separated
75g (3oz) caster sugar
75g (3oz) self-raising flour
150ml (5fl oz) double cream
Handful of very ripe soft fruits, such
*   as blackcurrants, strawberries,*
*   raspberries or redcurrants*
Icing sugar, sifted, for dusting

1 Preheat the oven to 160°C, 325°F, gas mark 3. Grease and line two 20cm (8in) round sandwich tins.

2 Whisk together the egg yolks and caster sugar in a large bowl until you have a very thick, pale and fluffy mixture.

3 In another, very clean bowl, whisk the egg whites until they are stiff. Fold the egg whites into the egg yolk mixture. Then sift the flour over the mixture and, with a very light touch, fold in the flour.

4 Divide the mixture evenly between the prepared tins and bake for 20 minutes until firm to the touch. Turn out onto a wire rack to cool.

5 Whip the cream until just thick. When the cakes are completely cold, spread the cream over one of the cakes, scatter the fruit over the cream and top with the second cake. Dust the top with a little icing sugar.

6 This cake is best eaten on the day it is made as it has no fat in the sponge so will dry out quickly.

All-in-one chocolate cake
20cm (8in) cake

225g (8oz) self-raising flour
400g (14oz) caster sugar
75g (3oz) cocoa powder
1½ teaspoons baking powder
1½ teaspoons bicarbonate of soda
2 large free-range eggs
250ml (9fl oz) milk
150ml (5fl oz) sunflower oil
2 teaspoons pure vanilla extract
125ml (4½fl oz) boiling water
100ml (4fl oz) double cream

1 Preheat the oven to 160°C, 325°F, gas mark 3. Grease and line two 20cm (8in) round sandwich tins.

2 Put all the ingredients except the double cream in a large bowl and beat together to a smooth, fairly thin batter.

3 Divide the mixture evenly between the prepared tins and bake for about 35 minutes until well risen and springy to the touch. Transfer to a wire rack to cool.

4 While the cakes are cooling, whip the cream until stiff.

5 When the cakes are completely cold, sandwich them together with whipped cream.

Cupcake and Biscuit Recipes

Simple cupcakes
12 cupcakes

100g (4oz) self-raising flour
100g (4oz) caster sugar
100g (4oz) margarine, softened
1 teaspoon baking powder
2 large free-range eggs
1 teaspoon pure vanilla extract

1   Preheat the oven to 160°C, 325°F, gas mark 3. Line a 12-hole muffin tin with baking papers.

2   Put all the ingredients into a mixer (food processor, food mixer, or just a large bowl with an electric whisk). Mix really well until the batter is light and fluffy.

3   Divide the mixture evenly among the prepared baking papers and bake in the oven for about 20 minutes until golden, firm and springy to the touch.

4   Remove from the oven and turn out onto a wire rack to cool. Add an icing of your choice to the top.

Basic butter biscuits
12–16 biscuits

250g (9oz) butter, softened
150g (5oz) icing sugar
1 teaspoon pure vanilla extract
1 large free-range egg yolk
375g (13oz) plain flour

1   Beat together the butter and sugar in a large bowl until very pale and fluffy. Add the vanilla and egg yolk and mix well. Sift in the flour and mix until it forms a firm dough. You may need to get your hands in here and work it into a smooth ball.

2   Wrap the dough in cling film and chill in the fridge for an hour. You can freeze it at this stage if you wish.

3   Preheat the oven to 190°C, 375°F, gas mark 5. Grease and line two baking sheets.

4   On a lightly floured surface, roll out the dough until it is about 3mm ($\frac{1}{8}$in) thick, then cut out the shapes you require and place on the prepared baking sheets. Bake for 10–12 minutes, or until the biscuits are pale golden.

5   Remove from the oven and transfer to a wire rack where they will harden as they cool.

Try adding chocolate chips or dried fruit pieces to simple shortbread.

Chocolate brownies
18 brownies

100g (4oz) unsalted butter
50g (2oz) dark chocolate (at least 70% cocoa solids)
2 large free-range eggs, lightly beaten
225g (8oz) caster sugar
50g (2oz) plain flour
100g (4oz) chopped walnuts

1 Preheat the oven to 180°C, 350°F, gas mark 4. Grease and line a 18 × 28cm (7 x 11in) cake tin.

2 Melt the butter and chocolate in a heatproof bowl over a pan of barely simmering water, but don't let the bottom of the bowl touch the water. Take the pan off the heat and let the mixture cool for about 5 minutes.

3 Tip it into a larger bowl, add all the remaining ingredients and beat well with a wooden spoon.

4 Turn the batter into the prepared cake tin and level the surface. Bake for about 30 minutes. The top will have crisped over but the middle will still be soggy – don't be afraid to take it out of the oven at that point, as it will continue to set as it cools. There's nothing worse than an overcooked brownie; you want a moist centre.

5 Remove from the oven and leave to cool in the tin before cutting it into squares or rectangles.

Simple shortbread
24 biscuits

250g (9oz) butter, softened
50g (2oz) caster sugar
250g (9oz) plain flour
125g (4½oz) cornflour

1 Preheat the oven to 160°C, 325°F, gas mark 3. Grease and line a 20cm (8in) square cake tin or a baking sheet.

2 Cream together the butter and sugar in a large bowl until light and fluffy. Sift the flour and cornflour onto the butter mixture and mix until you have a smooth dough.

3 If you are using a cake tin, press the dough into the prepared tin, then continue from step 4. Alternatively, to roll the dough, shape it into a fat sausage, wrap it in cling film and chill in the fridge for at least an hour. Unwrap the dough and slice into circles about 5mm (¼in) thick. Place on the prepared baking sheet.

4 Whichever method you choose, bake the shortbread for about 30–40 minutes until pale and golden.

5 Remove from the oven. Cut a large shortbread into pieces in the tin while it is still warm and leave to cool in the tin. Transfer rolled biscuits to a wire rack to cool.

Pastry Recipes

Flaky pastry
450g (1lb) pastry

450g (1lb) plain flour
1 teaspoon salt
350g (12oz) butter, or half butter and
  half lard, softened
1 teaspoon lemon juice
300ml (10fl oz) cold water

1   Mix together the flour and salt. Divide the fat into four portions. Rub one portion into the flour with your fingertips. Mix in the lemon juice and cold water to give a soft dough, and knead gently on a lightly floured surface until smooth.

2   Roll out the dough to a rectangle three times longer than it is wide. Dot the second portion of fat over the top two-thirds of the surface. Fold up the bottom third and fold down the top third and seal the edges. Wrap in cling film or a plastic bag and chill for 15 minutes.

3   Place the dough on the floured surface with the folded edges to your right and left, and roll out again to a rectangle. Repeat the dotting, folding and chilling process twice more until all the fat is used. Wrap again and chill for at least 45 minutes before using.

Puff pastry
450g (1lb) pastry

450g (1lb) plain flour
1 teaspoon salt
450g (1lb) butter, softened
1 teaspoon lemon juice
About 75–100ml (3–4fl oz) iced water

1   Mix together the flour and salt. Cut 25g (1oz) of the butter into small pieces, then rub it into the flour until the mixture resembles fine breadcrumbs. Add the lemon juice and enough water to give a soft dough. Knead lightly until really smooth.

2   In a clean linen cloth, shape the remaining butter into a rectangle. On a lightly floured surface, roll out the pastry to a rectangle slightly wider than the rectangle of butter and about twice its length.

3   Place the butter on one half of the pastry and fold the other half over. Press the edges together with a rolling pin. Leave in a cool place for 15 minutes to allow the butter to harden slightly.

4   Roll out the pastry to a long strip three times its original length, keeping the width the same. The corners should be square, the sides straight and the thickness even. The butter must not break through the dough. Fold the bottom third up and the top third down, press the edges together with a rolling pin, put inside a well-oiled plastic bag and chill for 30 minutes.

5   Place the dough on the floured board with the folded edges to your right and left, and roll out into a long strip as before. Fold again into three and chill for a further 30 minutes. Repeat this process four times more, then chill for 30 minutes before using.

Remember to keep everything cold when making pastry, even your hands!

Rough puff pastry
450g (1lb) pastry

450g (1lb) plain flour
A pinch of salt
350g (12oz) butter, softened
1 teaspoon lemon juice
3–4 tablespoons cold water

1 Mix together the flour and salt. Cut the butter into small pieces and stir lightly into the flour with a round-bladed knife. Make a well in the centre, add the lemon juice and mix with enough water to give an elastic dough.

2 On a lightly floured surface, roll out the dough to a long strip, keeping the sides straight and the corners square. Fold up the bottom third and fold down the top third then turn the dough so the folded edges are to your right and left.

3 Repeat the rolling and folding process three times more, chilling the pastry for 15 minutes between the third and fourth rolling. Chill for at least 15 minutes before using.

Rich shortcrust pastry
450g (1lb) pastry

450g (1lb) plain flour
A good pinch of salt
350g (12oz) butter, softened
2 large free-range egg yolks
4 teaspoons caster sugar
3–4 tablespoons cold water

1 Mix together the flour and salt. Rub in the butter until the mixture resembles breadcrumbs. Make a well in the centre, add the egg yolks and sugar and mix with a round-bladed knife. Add enough of the water, a little at a time, to give a stiff but pliable dough. Knead lightly until smooth.

2 Wrap in cling film or a plastic bag and chill in the fridge for at least 15 minutes before using.

Shortcrust pastry
450g (1lb) pastry

450g (1lb) plain flour
A pinch of salt
100g (4oz) butter, softened
100g (4oz) lard or vegetable
   shortening, softened
3–4 tablespoons cold water

1 Mix together the flour and salt. Cut the fats into small pieces and rub into the flour until the mixture resembles breadcrumbs.

2 Gradually add enough water, mixing with a fork, to give a stiff but pliable dough. Knead lightly until smooth.

3 Wrap in cling film or a plastic bag and chill for at least 15 minutes before using.

It is important to chill pastry dough before using so that it doesn't shrink when baking.

The Icing on the Cake

Here are three very straightforward types of icing that you can easily make to decorate your cakes and biscuits. Glacé icing is made simply with water or lemon juice. It's a question of sieving the icing sugar, adding the liquid and stirring. That's it. The second icing is buttercream. Butter, sifted icing sugar, and stir. Flavours, colours and embellishments may be added, but they are simple.

Even simpler is spreading something on top of a cake or muffin straight out of a jar or tub. Why not? Chocolate spread, lemon curd, mascarpone, whipped double cream – all of these would make delicious additions. It is worth remembering, however, that low in effort doesn't actually mean low in cost.

For cakes that involve a bit more fiddling and twiddling and where you have to make some decorations in advance, rolled fondant icing is the order of the day. Fondant is made with icing sugar which generally has had some dried glycerine added to it. It's versatile, easy to handle and comes in a wide range of colours. Roll it or shape it and mould it into animals, flowers, patterns, or anything else suitable to the occasion.

You will see that some of the cakes – particularly those in the chapter Fun for Little Ones – use food colourings for some

fun decorative effects. You may be happy with this. However, if you prefer to avoid non-natural substances in your food, then you will need to look into this in some more detail. Really bright colours are rarely entirely natural.

Having said that, there are companies out there who produce quite a range of tartrazine-free colours so ask in store or look online for suitable products.

Gels are much better than the liquids to colour your icing. They don't thin the icing and the colours tend to be much more versatile. You can get them from good kitchen shops and sugarcraft specialists. A word of warning here: a little goes a long way.

Glacé icing
Enough for 12 cupcakes

This is the simplest and most useful icing. Minimum ingredients and minimum fuss. It is very easily correctible if you make it too thick or too thin.

200g (7oz) icing sugar, sifted
Juice of 1 large lemon OR 4
  tablespoons boiling water
Gel food colouring of your choice

1 Put the sifted icing sugar in a bowl. Gradually begin to add the liquid a little at a time, stirring continuously until smooth and a little thicker than double cream.

2 Add a tiny amount of food colouring if you wish, using a cocktail stick dipped into the colour. Add it gradually so that you do not overdo the colour. Finally, add a little more icing sugar if necessary so that the consistency is fairly firm.

Buttercream
Enough for 12 cupcakes

This sweet, melt-in-the-mouth icing is equally delicious as a filling between layers of cake. Just make sure you beat it really well so that it is light and fluffy.

225g (8oz) icing sugar, sifted
100g (4oz) soft unsalted butter
½ teaspoon pure vanilla extract
   (optional)

1 Beat everything together in a large bowl for a few minutes until light and fluffy. If the mixture looks a little on the heavy side, whisk in ½ teaspoon boiling water.

2 If you want coloured or flavoured buttercream, try some of the suggestions on the right, or experiment with your own ideas.

Royal icing
Enough for 24 cupcakes

This is a great icing to use for decorating cakes, and you are aiming for an icing that holds peaks like a meringue. It is not difficult, but it can take a little practise as you need to watch the consistency.

2 large free-range egg whites
500g (1lb 2oz) icing sugar, sifted
2 teaspoons freshly squeezed lemon
   juice

1 Put everything into a large mixing bowl, and whisk for 4–5 minutes until the mixture is very white and standing in stiff peaks. It should be quite stiff. If the mixture is too stiff, add a few extra drops of lemon juice or boiling water. If it is too runny, gradually add a little more sifted icing sugar.

2 This makes quite a large amount, so you may wish to halve the quantity, but it does keep well for about a week in the fridge if you seal it really well. Cover the top closely with cling film, then seal in an airtight plastic container.

Tasty buttercream

COFFEE
Mix into the buttercream:
1 teaspoon extremely strong espresso or filter coffee (made with instant coffee – 3 teaspoons coffee granules with just enough boiling water to make it liquid).

CHOCOLATE
Mix into the buttercream:
2–3 teaspoons sifted cocoa powder. If you are feeling very extravagant, melt 50g (2oz) good-quality plain chocolate (at least 70% cocoa solids) in a bowl over a pan of simmering water, and mix thoroughly into the buttercream.

LEMON OR CITRUS
Mix into the buttercream:
grated zest of 1 unwaxed lemon
2 teaspoons lemon juice.
This also works well with limes or oranges.

ROSE
Mix into the buttercream:
1 teaspoon rosewater, or more to taste.
Do not confuse rosewater with rose extract: the latter is very powerful and you'll only need one or two tiny drops in your buttercream.

If you don't want to make your own icing, there are plenty of different types available to buy

Traditional *Favourites*

Victoria Sponge

20cm
(8in)
cake

The mother of all everyday cakes, a Victoria sponge is like the comforting, faithful friend of the cake world. The house smells gorgeous when it's in the oven, it is easy to make and you can vary it by changing the jam in the centre, adding buttercream, fresh cream, luscious strawberries or raspberries when they are at their best – the possibilities are endless.

175g (6oz) caster sugar, plus extra
  to decorate
175g (6oz) soft margarine
3 large free-range eggs
175g (6oz) self-raising flour
4 tablespoons raspberry jam

1 Preheat the oven to 180°C, 350°F, gas mark 4. Grease and line two 20cm (8in) round sandwich tins.

2 Put the sugar and margarine in a large bowl and beat well using a freestanding mixer or an electric hand whisk until light and fluffy. Beat the eggs in little by little. Fold the sifted flour into the mixture.

3 Divide the mixture evenly between the prepared tins and level the tops. Bake for about 20 minutes. The cakes should be springy to the touch and a skewer inserted into the centre should come out clean.

4 Remove from the oven, cool in the tin for five minutes then turn out onto a wire rack to cool completely.

5 When the cakes are completely cool, sandwich them together with the jam, and dust the top with a little more caster sugar.

Light Sponge Cake

20cm (8in) cake

This recipe is originally from Chirk Castle in Wales, where afternoon tea was an elegant but small meal of sandwiches the size of a postage stamp. In cold weather a dish of hot buttered muffins or warm scones was also served. One footman, who used to take tea into the salon, once said, 'When clearing away, I always remember you had to eat at least four sandwiches to even taste them!'

200g (7oz) granulated or
   caster sugar
2 large free-range eggs
150g (5oz) self-raising flour
A pinch of salt
1 teaspoon baking powder
50g (2oz) butter
100ml (4fl oz) milk
2–3 drops pure vanilla extract
150ml (5fl oz) double cream
100g (4oz) soft fruits, such as
   strawberries and raspberries
Icing sugar, sifted, for dusting

1 Preheat the oven to 160°C, 325°F, gas mark 3. Grease and line a 20cm (8in) round cake tin.

2 Beat together the sugar and eggs in a large bowl until thick and creamy. Add the flour, salt and baking powder and mix well.

3 Put the milk in a small pan and heat gently. Melt the butter in the milk and bring to the boil. When boiling, add to the flour mixture with the vanilla extract, and beat well until smooth and runny.

4 Turn into the prepared tin and bang the pan sharply on the table to remove the air bubbles. Bake for 20–25 minutes until a skewer inserted into the centre comes out clean.

5 Remove from the oven and leave to cool in the tin for 15 minutes before turning out onto a wire rack to cool completely.

6 Whisk the cream until stiff. Slice the cake in half horizontally. Spread the bottom half with the cream, then the fruit, then top with the other half of the cake. Dust with icing sugar to serve.

This cake is quick and easy to make, and is delicious served with fruit and cream. It is ideal for freezing.

Everyday Coffee Cake

20cm (8in) cake

The key to making the perfect coffee cake is to use a really strong coffee so that you get plenty of flavour in the finished cake. An alternative to the recipe below could be to make only half the quantity of buttercream and use it to sandwich the cake, then dust the top with a little icing sugar sifted with instant coffee powder. The walnuts on top are also optional.

175g (6oz) self-raising flour
175g (6oz) caster sugar
175g (6oz) soft margarine
3 large free-range eggs
8 heaped teaspoons instant coffee granules
3 teaspoons boiling water

For the filling and topping
150g (5½oz) unsalted butter
400g (14oz) icing sugar, sifted
8 walnut halves

1 Preheat the oven to 160°C, 325°F, gas mark 3. Grease and line two 20cm (8in) round sandwich tins.

2 Beat together the flour, caster sugar, margarine and eggs until they are very light and fluffy, preferably in an electric mixer.

3 Put the coffee granules in a cup or small bowl and add about 3 teaspoons boiling water. The coffee should be very, very dark and just runny – if it's a bit stiff, add a few drops more water, but it certainly shouldn't look like ordinary coffee. You want a liquor that will give a huge hit of coffee without adding too much volume of liquid.

4 Add 1 teaspoon coffee mixture to the cake mix and beat it in. Taste, and add more coffee if needed. Don't throw away any remaining mixture.

5 Divide the batter evenly between the prepared tins and smooth the tops. Bake for 20 minutes until the cakes are firm and springy to the touch.

6 Remove from the oven and turn out onto a wire rack to cool.

7 To make the filling, beat together the butter and 150g (5oz) icing sugar until pale and soft. Add 1 teaspoon coffee mixture and taste. Add more, to taste, or add icing sugar if the buttercream is too soft.

8 In another bowl, add the remaining coffee mixture to the remaining icing sugar and mix until you have a smooth mixture with the consistency of custard. If it's too runny, add more icing sugar; if too thick, add a drop of water.

9 When the sponges are cold, sandwich them together with the buttercream and then frost the top of the cake with the coffee icing. Place the walnuts around the edge of the cake and leave the icing to set, which should only take about an hour.

Simnel Cake

20cm (8in) cake

This rich fruit cake – with its hidden layer of marzipan in the centre – is traditionally made at Easter. The eleven balls of marzipan on the top of the cake symbolise the eleven faithful apostles, omitting Judas. The golden effect on the marzipan is created by flashing the cake under a hot grill.

550g (1lb 4oz) marzipan
Icing sugar, sifted, for dusting
175g (6oz) butter, softened
150g (5oz) light soft brown sugar
3 large free-range eggs, beaten
15g (½ oz) glycerine
15g (½ oz) liquid glucose
100g (4oz) strong plain flour
50g (2oz) white plain flour
25g (1oz) ground almonds
1 teaspoon mixed spice
½ teaspoon freshly grated nutmeg
350g (12oz) sultanas
250g (9oz) currants
100g (4oz) chopped mixed peel
A little sieved apricot jam for fixing the marzipan topping in place

1 Preheat the oven to 180°C, 350°F, gas mark 4. Grease and double line a 20cm (8in) round cake tin.

2 Divide the marzipan into three portions, one slightly smaller than the other two. Set the smallest portion aside. Dust the surface with icing sugar and roll out one of the two equal portions to a circle just smaller than the diameter of the tin.

3 Beat together the butter and sugar in a large bowl until light and fluffy. Add the beaten eggs, glycerine and glucose, and beat again. Mix together the flours, almonds and spices, and gradually add to the mixture, stirring gently to blend. Do not beat. Gently fold in the dried fruit.

4 Turn half the batter into the prepared cake tin and smooth the top. Put the marzipan circle on top, cover with the remaining batter and smooth the top. Bake for 1 hour (if the top starts to become too brown, cover with a double layer of baking paper), then reduce the oven temperature to

160°C, 325°F, gas mark 3 and bake for another 45–55 minutes until a skewer inserted into the centre comes out clean.

5 Remove from the oven and leave to cool in the tin for about 15 minutes before turning out onto a wire rack to cool completely.

6 When the cake is completely cold, brush the top with apricot jam. Roll out the second portion of marzipan into a circle to fit the top of the cake. Press gently into place. Form the remaining marzipan into eleven small balls and arrange them around the rim of the cake, sticking them on with a little apricot jam. Turn the grill to a moderate heat and place the cake underneath for a few minutes until the marzipan just begins to turn a golden brown.

7 To serve, wrap a wide yellow satin ribbon around the cake and fix with a pin. Arrange a small posy of fresh spring flowers on the top.

Perfect for lovers of marzipan, Simnel cake has a secret layer of it within the cake as well as the top decoration.

Basic Chocolate Cake

20cm (8in) cake

This is a no-nonsense chocolate sponge sandwich: light, moist and delicious yet so easy to make and bake in scarcely any time at all. To make sure it tastes really great, though, do make sure you use the best-quality cocoa powder. When a recipe is simple, the quality of the ingredients come into the spotlight, so this is not a time to cut corners.

150g (5oz) self-raising flour
175g (6oz) caster sugar
175g (6oz) soft margarine
3 large free-range eggs
1 tablespoon milk
50g (2oz) good-quality cocoa
    powder, sifted
100g (4oz) unsalted butter
200g (7oz) icing sugar, sifted
1–2 teaspoons milk (optional)
Chocolate buttons to decorate
    (optional)

1 Preheat the oven to 160°C, 325°F, gas mark 3. Grease and line two 20cm (8in) round sandwich tins.

2 Beat together the flour, caster sugar, margarine, eggs, milk and half the cocoa powder, preferably in an electric mixer. Beat for about 2 minutes until the batter is pale brown and fluffy.

3 Divide the mixture evenly between the prepared tins and smooth the tops. Bake for about 20 minutes until the tops of the cakes are firm and springy to the touch.

4 Remove from the oven and turn out onto a wire rack to cool.

5 While the cakes are cooling, make the buttercream. Beat together the butter, icing sugar and remaining cocoa until soft and fluffy. If necessary, add 1 teaspoon or so of milk to get a softer consistency – you need to be able to spread this.

6 When the cakes are completely cold, sandwich them together with half the buttercream and spread the remaining buttercream on the top of the cake. Decorate, if you wish, with chocolate buttons or any other chocolate that takes your fancy.

Easy Fruit Cake

20cm (8in) cake

A bad fruit cake can be very disappointing, so all the more reason to make sure you use a tried-and-tested recipe like this one to be confident you'll get a good result. This is an everyday boiled cake that is ideal to serve with a cup of tea. It also keeps well in an airtight container. You could even use it for a Christmas recipe, perhaps adding a little brandy to the mixture.

100g (4oz) raisins
100g (4oz) ready-to-eat dried apricots
50g (2oz) dried cherries
100g (4oz) dried peaches (or pears)
150ml (5fl oz) water
100g (4oz) unsalted butter
100g (4oz) dark brown sugar
2 large free-range eggs, beaten
1 teaspoon mixed spice
225g (8oz) self-raising flour

1 Preheat the oven to 150°C, 300°F, gas mark 2. Grease and line a 20cm (8in) cake tin.

2 Put the dried fruit, water, butter and sugar into a pan and heat gently until the mixture comes up to simmering point. Simmer for about 20 minutes, giving it a stir every now and again to stop the mixture sticking. Leave the mixture to cool (if you add the eggs while it's too hot you will get scrambled eggs).

3 When the mixture is cool, add the eggs and spice and sift the flour over the top. Mix well with a wooden spoon.

4 Turn the batter into the prepared tin and smooth the top. Make a small indent in the centre of the cake to prevent it doming. Bake for about 1–1½ hours until a skewer inserted into the centre comes out clean. Check after 1 hour and if it needs longer in the oven and the top is getting too brown, cover it with baking parchment.

5 Remove from the oven and leave the cake to cool in the tin for about 20 minutes before turning out onto a wire rack to cool completely.

Carrot Cake with Lime Topping

This indulgent cake is best eaten with pastry forks. These three-pronged tea forks developed from Victorian dessert forks in the second half of the 19th century. So that pressure could be exerted on a fruit tartlet, the first two narrow prongs were fused to make a wider prong that acted as a cutting edge. Like tea knives and silver teaspoons, they usually came in boxes of six.

For the cake
2 large free-range eggs
100g (4oz) light soft brown sugar
5 tablespoons oil (sunflower, vegetable or corn)
100g (4oz) self-raising flour
175g (6oz) carrots, grated
1 teaspoon ground cinnamon
50g (2oz) shredded coconut

For the topping
75g (3oz) cream cheese
75g (3oz) butter
50g (2oz) icing sugar
Grated zest of 1 lime
Toasted coconut and grated lime, to decorate (optional)

1 Preheat the oven to 190°C, 375°F, gas mark 5. Grease and line an 18cm (7in) round cake tin or a 900g (2lb) loaf tin.

2 Beat together the eggs and sugar in a large bowl until very creamy. Add the oil and beat hard. Fold in the remaining ingredients.

3 Turn into the prepared tin and smooth the top, then slightly hollow out the centre to avoid a very domed top on the finished cake.

4 Bake for 35–40 minutes until golden and well risen and a skewer inserted in the centre comes out clean. Remove from the oven and turn out onto a wire rack to cool.

5 To make the topping, beat the ingredients together until light and creamy, and spread over the top of the cake. Make a pattern with the prongs of a fork, then decorate with the coconut and lime.

For a more traditional carrot cake, simply leave the lime and coconut out of the topping.

Sunday Best Chocolate Cake

20cm (8in) cake

A sumptuous cake for special occasions. The ingredients include two sorts of chocolate – cocoa powder and white chocolate. Cocoa powder is made by grinding down the seeds found inside cocoa pods into a thick creamy paste and then separating the cocoa butter from the cocoa solids. The cocoa butter is used as the basis for rich, creamy white chocolate.

For the cake
225g (8oz) plain wholemeal flour
5 teaspoons baking powder
225g (8oz) butter, softened
225g (8oz) light or dark
    soft brown sugar
5 large free-range eggs, beaten
3 tablespoons cocoa powder, sifted

For the filling and topping
300ml (10fl oz) double cream
675g (1lb 9oz) white chocolate,
    grated
Grated dark chocolate, curls of
    white chocolate or chocolate
    buttons, to decorate

1 Preheat the oven to 160°C, 325°F, gas mark 3. Grease and line three 20cm (8in) round sandwich tins.

2 Place all the ingredients for the cake in a large bowl and beat thoroughly to give a soft, dropping consistency (add a little water if it is too dry).

3 Divide the mixture equally between the prepared tins and smooth the tops. Bake for about 30 minutes until the sponge springs back when lightly pressed.

4 Remove from the oven and turn out onto a wire rack to cool.

5 To make the filling, bring the cream just to boiling point in a heavy pan and stir in the chocolate. Remove from the heat and stir until well blended. Leave in a cool place until it reaches spreading consistency.

6 Use the filling to sandwich the cakes together and to cover the top and sides of the cake. Decorate with grated dark chocolate, fat curls of white chocolate or chocolate buttons.

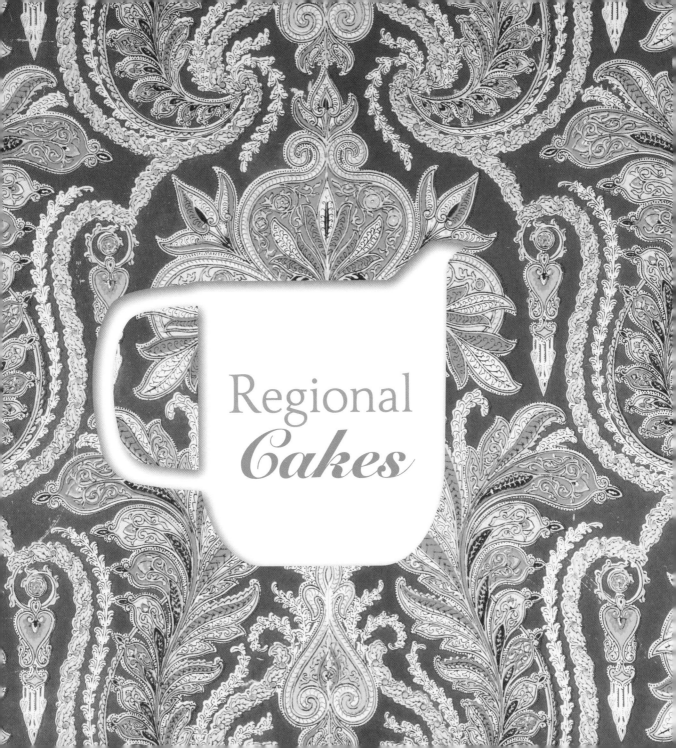

Regional
Cakes

Suffolk Fourses

During the annual harvest in England's eastern counties, the farmers' wives produced four or five meals a day to feed the hungry local and itinerant workers. At midday and mid-afternoon, the women and children carried out flasks of tea and bottles of homemade lemonade. Everyone stopped and found a shady place to rest and devour the freshly baked breads, rolls and cakes.

25g (1oz) fresh yeast (to substitute dried yeast, see page 216)
1 teaspoon caster sugar
300ml (10fl oz) milk
900g (2lb) strong white bread flour
½ teaspoon salt
50g (2oz) lard or vegetable shortening, softened
100g (4oz) caster, granulated or demerara sugar
100g (4oz) currants or raisins
A pinch of mixed spice
175g (6oz) butter, melted and cooled
3 large free-range eggs, well beaten
Caster or demerara sugar for dredging

1 Cream the yeast with 1 teaspoon of caster sugar. Warm the milk to blood heat and add to the yeast. Leave to one side.

2 Mix together the flour and salt and rub in the fat. Add the sugar, currants or raisins and spice and mix well.

3 Stir the melted butter into the beaten eggs. Add to the milk and yeast mixture, then pour into the flour. Mix with a round-bladed knife to a light dough. Cover the bowl with a clean damp cloth and leave in a warm place for 2 hours until the dough has doubled in size.

4 Meanwhile, grease two baking sheets. When the dough has risen, knead on a lightly floured surface, then roll out to a thickness of 1.5cm (¾in) and cut into circles 10cm (4in) in diameter. Place on the prepared baking sheets and leave to rise in a warm place for 30 minutes.

5 Preheat the oven to 200°C, 400°F, gas mark 6.

6 When the fourses have risen, mark the tops into four sections and dredge with caster or demerara sugar. Bake for 15–20 minutes until firm and golden.

7 Remove from the oven and eat either warm or cold, split in half and buttered.

Bath Buns

20 buns

In the 18th century, these local treats were flavoured with sherry, rose water and caraway seeds. The more modern version uses chopped mixed peel and currants, and is topped with the characteristic crushed lump sugar, which gives the buns their distinctive crunchy quality.

25g (1oz) fresh yeast (to substitute dried yeast, see page 216)
100g (4oz) caster sugar
550g (1lb 4oz) strong white bread flour
150ml (5fl oz) milk, warmed
A pinch of salt
175g (6oz) currants and sultanas, mixed
50g (2oz) chopped mixed peel
50g (2oz) butter, melted
2 large free-range eggs, beaten
Crushed sugar lump for sprinkling

1 In a medium-sized bowl, cream the yeast with 1 teaspoon of the sugar. Add 50g (2oz) of the flour and the warmed milk and mix to a thick batter. Leave in a warm place for 15–20 minutes until frothy.

2 Mix together the remaining flour and the salt. Add the remaining caster sugar, currants, sultanas and mixed peel. Add to the yeast mixture with the melted butter and most of the beaten eggs (reserving a little for glazing) and mix to a soft dough. Knead on a lightly floured surface for 2–3 minutes until smooth.

3 Place the dough in a lightly floured bowl, cover with a damp cloth and leave in a warm place to rise for 1½–1¾ hours until doubled in size.

4 Grease two baking sheets. Knock back the dough and form into 20 bun shapes. Place well apart on the prepared baking sheets, cover with oiled cling film and leave to rise for about 30 minutes until doubled in size.

5 Preheat the oven to 190°C, 375°F, gas mark 5.

6 Glaze the buns with the remaining beaten egg and sprinkle with the crushed sugar. Bake for 15 minutes until well risen and golden. Remove from the oven and transfer to a wire rack to cool.

Cornish Splits

Cooks and maids in the vast kitchens of Lanhydrock made bread, splits, cakes and biscuits for family teas in the morning room. Covered in a lace cloth, the table was set with French china cups and saucers, silver tea knives and spoons, linen napkins, a beehive honey pot and a silver jam pot and butter dish.

50g (2oz) fresh yeast (to substitute dried yeast, see page 216)
40g (1½oz) caster sugar
Just under 600ml (1 pint) warm milk and water, mixed
900g (2lb) strong white bread flour
1 large free-range egg, beaten
Jam, clotted cream and icing sugar, dusted, to serve

1 Grease two baking sheets. Mix together the yeast, sugar and warm milk and water. Leave in a warm place for about 20–30 minutes until frothy.

2 Add the liquid to the flour with the beaten egg and mix to a soft dough. Knead until smooth and elastic. Leave in a warm place for about an hour until doubled in size.

3 Knock back the dough, knead again and divide into 12 pieces. Mould with your hands into neat bun shapes, place on the prepared baking sheets, cover with a damp cloth and leave in a warm place for about 20 minutes until well risen.

4 Preheat the oven to 160°C, 325°F, gas mark 3. When the splits are well risen, bake for 20–25 minutes until they just start to turn brown.

5 Remove from the oven and transfer to a wire rack to cool. To serve, split and fill with jam and clotted cream, and dust the tops with icing sugar.

Cherry Bakewell Tarts

Originally called Bakewell puddings, Bakewell tarts are said to date back to the 16th century and to have been invented by accident when a cook at a local inn misunderstood her employer's instructions to make a strawberry tart. Instead of adding eggs and sugar to the pastry, she beat them with a secret ingredient and spread the mixture over the strawberries.

225g (8oz) shortcrust pastry
(see page 15)
50g (2oz) strawberry jam
100g (4oz) butter, softened
100g (4oz) caster sugar
2 large free-range eggs
50g (2oz) ground almonds
50g (2oz) self-raising flour
1 teaspoon almond extract
175g (6oz) icing sugar, sifted
1–2 tablespoons water
20 cherries (fresh, stoned or glacé)

1 Make the pastry according to the instructions on page 15 and chill for at least 15 minutes.

2 Preheat the oven to 200°C, 400°F, gas mark 6. Grease 20 cupcake tins.

3 On a lightly floured surface, roll out the pastry and cut 20 circles using a 7.5 cm (3 in) cutter. Use to line the prepared tins and spread a little jam in the base of each.

4 Beat together the butter and caster sugar, then beat in the eggs, one at a time, adding half the ground almonds after each one. Add the flour and almond extract, and stir well.

5 Spoon the batter into the pastry cases and bake for 20 minutes until well risen, firm and golden. Remove from the oven and leave to cool in the tins.

6 Mix together the icing sugar and enough water to make a thick icing and, when the tarts are cold, spoon the icing on the top. Decorate each one with a cherry.

18th-century Pepper Cake

23cm
(9in)
cake

Although generally used in savoury dishes, black pepper is sometimes added to cakes with ginger and other spices. Some recipes for this traditional Westmorland fruit cake also add dates and walnuts, but this one, originally from Wordsworth House in the Lake District uses cloves, currants, raisins and peel.

450g (1lb) plain flour
1 teaspoon baking powder
100g (4oz) butter, softened
225g (8oz) caster sugar
100g (4oz) currants
100g (4oz) raisins
25g (1oz) mixed candied peel
½ teaspoon ground cloves
½ teaspoon ground ginger
½ teaspoon ground black pepper
225g (8oz) black treacle
4 large free-range eggs, beaten

1 Preheat the oven to 150°C, 300°F, gas mark 2. Grease and line a 23cm (9in) round, deep cake tin.

2 Mix together the flour and baking powder and rub in the butter until the mixture resembles fine breadcrumbs. Add all the other ingredients and mix to a thick batter. Turn the batter into the prepared tin and bake for 2 hours until a skewer inserted in the centre comes out clean.

3 Remove from the oven and leave to cool in the tin for 15 minutes before turning out onto a wire rack to cool completely.

4 When cool, wrap in foil or cling film and store for a few days before eating.

Welsh Cakes

These little flat spicy griddle cakes were often offered to visitors. They were traditionally cooked on a bakestone that sat on the open kitchen fire – their Welsh name is 'pice ary maen', meaning 'cakes on the stone'. The Llech Cymraeg variation is made with plain flour to give a flatter, crisper cake, and Jam Split is made by cutting the Welsh cake across the centre and filling it with jam.

225g (8oz) self-raising flour
A pinch of salt
50g (2oz) lard or vegetable shortening, softened
50g (2oz) butter, softened
75g (3oz) granulated sugar
25g (1oz) currants
½ large free-range egg, beaten
1½ tablespoons milk
Caster sugar for sprinkling

1 Preheat a griddle or a heavy frying pan to a medium, even temperature.

2 Mix together the flour and salt and rub in the fat. Add the sugar and currants, and mix with the egg and milk to a soft dough.

3 On a lightly floured surface, roll out to a thickness of 5mm–1cm (¼–½in) and cut out circles using a 7.5cm (3in) cutter. Place on the griddle and cook both sides until light golden. Lift onto a wire rack to cool and sprinkle with caster sugar before serving.

Welsh cakes are quick to make and taste wonderful served warm from the griddle with a steaming cup of tea.

Banbury Cakes

Banbury cakes date back to pagan days and are thought to have been eaten at May Day celebrations. Recipes have changed greatly over the centuries, varying from a type of fruited bread flavoured with caraway seeds, to pastry cases filled with fruit, saffron and sherry. Today's cakes are a fruit-filled pastry with a flaky outer case and plump dried fruit inside.

350g (12oz) puff pastry
  (see page 14)
50g (2oz) butter
100g (4oz) currants
50g (2oz) chopped mixed peel
¼ teaspoon ground cinnamon
½ teaspoon allspice or freshly grated
  nutmeg
2½ tablespoons light or dark soft
  brown sugar
1 tablespoon dark rum
A little milk or water
1 large free-range egg white, lightly
  beaten
Caster sugar for dredging

1 Make the pastry according to the instructions on page 14 and chill for at least 30 minutes.

2 Melt the butter in a small pan and add the dried fruit, spices, brown sugar and rum. Stir and leave to cool.

3 Preheat the oven to 230°F, 450°F, gas mark 8. Grease two baking sheets.

4 On a lightly floured surface, roll out the pastry to a thickness of 5mm (¼in) and cut into circles about 10cm (4in) in diameter.

5 Place a spoonful of the fruit mixture onto each circle, dampen the edges of the pastry with a little milk or water and gather the edges together. Seal well, turn each cake over and roll gently to a neat oval shape. Cut three slashes in the top and place on the prepared baking sheets.

6 Brush the tops with the beaten egg white and dredge with caster sugar. Bake for 10–15 minutes until golden. Remove from the oven and transfer to a wire rack to cool slightly before serving.

Kedleston Marmalade Cake

20cm (8in) cake

Marmalades started life as a sort of quince (marmelo) jam but, in the 17th century, were made in England with oranges instead. This recipe is originally from the kitchens of the 18th century neo-classical Kedleston Hall in Derbyshire. The bittersweet flavour adds an interesting bite to this cake which goes very well with Ceylon or Assam tea.

175g (6oz) butter, softened
50g (2oz) light or dark soft brown sugar
4 tablespoons golden syrup
2 large free-range eggs
250g (5oz) orange marmalade
275g (10oz) self-raising wholemeal flour
2 teaspoons baking powder
½ teaspoon ground ginger
3–4 tablespoons orange juice
Icing sugar, sifted, for dusting

1 Preheat the oven to 180°C, 350°F, gas mark 4. Grease and line a 20cm (8in) round cake tin.

2 Beat together the butter and sugar until light and fluffy. Add the syrup and beat again.

3 Whisk together the eggs and marmalade and add to the mixture with the flour, baking powder and ginger. Stir in the orange juice to give a soft, dropping consistency.

4 Turn the batter into the prepared tin and bake for about 1 hour until a skewer inserted in the centre comes out clean.

5 Remove from the oven and leave to cool in the tin for 15 minutes before turning out onto a wire rack to cool completely. Dust with icing sugar, to serve.

If you want to dress up this cake, try making an orange glacé icing to drizzle over the top.

Ultimate Tarts

The tart is another British teatime staple, and every region has its own take on a pastry case filled with something sweet and delicious.

Treacle Tart
25cm (10in) tart

Beningbrough Hall near York has served this sticky, indulgent tart in its tearoom. The house, built in 1716, has a private closet on the ground floor as part of a grand suite of rooms used by honoured guests. Richly decorated, the closet was used to entertain visitors to tea and all the essential porcelain teapots, bowls and dishes for brewing and serving tea were displayed on shelves and ledges over the fireplace. The tea was too expensive to leave in charge of the servants so it was kept here in little porcelain jars imported from China. The jars gradually changed shape and became squat, hinge-lidded tea caddies.

For the pastry
50g (2oz) lard or other shortening, softened
50g (2oz) butter, softened
225g (8oz) plain flour
25g (1oz) caster sugar
A little cold water

For the filling
450g (1lb) golden syrup
100–175g (4–6oz) fresh white breadcrumbs
Juice of ½ lemon

1 To make the pastry, rub the fats into the flour to a coarse crumb. Add the sugar and enough water to mix to a soft but pliable dough. Knead lightly, wrap in cling film and chill in the fridge for at least 15 minutes.

2 Preheat the oven to 180°C, 350°F, gas mark 4. Lightly grease a 25cm (10in) round flan dish.

3 On a floured surface, roll out the pastry to fit the prepared dish and then use to line the base and sides.

4 To make the filling, put the golden syrup in a pan and warm gently. Remove from the heat, add the breadcrumbs and lemon juice, and leave until the bread is well soaked. If the mixture is dry, add a little more syrup. Turn the mixture into the pastry case and spread evenly. Bake for 25–30 minutes until the pastry is golden and the filling nicely browned. Remove from the oven and serve warm or cold.

Yorkshire Curd Tart
20cm (8in) tart

Open curd-cheese tarts and cheesecakes have been favourite puddings in Yorkshire for centuries and were often served as Easter specialities to use up some of the plentiful eggs and curd cheese available after the Lenten fast.

175g (6oz) shortcrust pastry
  (see page 15)
50g (2oz) butter, softened
50g (2oz) caster sugar
1 large free-range egg, beaten
50g (2oz) currants
100 g (4oz) cottage cheese
50g (2oz) sponge or biscuit crumbs
Grated zest and juice of 1 unwaxed lemon
½ teaspoon freshly grated nutmeg

1 Make the pastry according to the instructions on page 15 and chill for at least 15 minutes.

2 Preheat the oven to 190°C, 375°F, gas mark 5. Grease a 20cm (8in) round flan dish or tin.

3 On a floured surface, roll out the pastry to fit the dish and use to line the base and sides.

4 Beat together the butter and sugar until light and fluffy. Add the beaten egg and beat hard. Add the currants, cheese, sponge or biscuit crumbs, lemon zest and juice and the nutmeg and beat again. Turn into the pastry case and smooth the top. Bake for 20–25 minutes until golden.

5 Remove from the oven and leave to cool in the tin. Serve warm or cold with cream, if you like.

Longshaw Tart
25 × 30cm (10 × 12in) tart

Named after the estate near Sheffield where this recipe comes from, the tart is a version of Bakewell Tart, another local speciality. This may well have featured on the 'high tea' table when the family arrived home hungry at the end of the working day. Whereas 'afternoon tea' was also called 'low tea' (because one sat in low armchairs and chaises longues) or 'handed tea' (because the cups of tea were handed around by the hostess), 'high tea' was called 'meat tea' and 'great tea'.

350g (12oz) shortcrust pastry
  (see page 15)
6–7 tablespoons jam (raspberry,
  strawberry or apricot)
250g (9oz) butter, softened
225g (8oz) granulated sugar
115g (4½oz) peanuts, finely chopped
115g (4½oz) fresh breadcrumbs
  (white or wholemeal)
3 large free-range eggs, beaten
1½ teaspoons almond extract

1 Make the pastry according to the instructions on page 15 and chill for at least 15 minutes.

2 Preheat the oven to 190°C, 375°F, gas mark 5. Grease a 25 x 30 x 4cm (10 x 12 x 1½in) tin.

3 On a floured surface, roll out the pastry to make a rectangle to fit the tin and use to line the base and sides. Spread the jam over the pastry.

4 Beat together the butter and sugar until light and fluffy. Add the rest of the ingredients and mix well. Turn into the pastry case and bake for 25–30 minutes until firm and golden.

5 Remove from the oven and leave to cool in the tin. When cold, cut into slices and lift carefully out of the tin.

Secretary tarts
24 individual tarts

These oddly named tartlets are served in the tearoom at Polesden Lacey in Surrey – a Regency house with strong links to afternoon tea rituals. Hosted by Mrs Ronnie Greville, the elegant society hostess, tea was an important part of the famous parties held from 1906 until the outbreak of World War II. Guests included Indian maharajahs, literary figures such as Beverley Nichols and Harold Nicolson, prominent politicians and royalty, including Edward VII. The future George VI and Queen Elizabeth even honeymooned here.

450g (1lb) rich shortcrust or shortcrust pastry (see page 15)
175g (6oz) butter
175g (6oz) light soft brown sugar
400g (14oz) can condensed milk
50g (2oz) walnuts, roughly chopped
50g (2oz) raisins

1 Make the pastry according to the instructions on page 15 and chill for at least 15 minutes.

2 Preheat the oven to 230°F, 450°F, gas mark 8. Grease 24 cupcake tins.

3 On a lightly floured surface, roll out the pastry to a thickness of 5mm (¼in) and cut 24 circles using a 7.5cm (3in) fluted cutter. Use to line the prepared cupcake tins. Place little squares of baking paper in each tart and fill with baking beans. Bake blind for 10 minutes.

4 Remove the pastry cases from the oven, lift the baking beans and paper out of the cases and return to the oven for a further 5 minutes. Remove and turn off the oven.

5 Put the butter, sugar and milk into a medium-sized pan and bring to the boil. Boil hard for 7 minutes, stirring all the time, until the mixture becomes a caramel colour. Remove from the heat and allow to cool for 5 minutes. Stir in the walnuts and raisins and spoon into the pastry cases. Put into the fridge to set. Serve cold.

Most tart recipes can be adapted to make dainty individual tarts. Just watch the baking time and oven temperature – you may need to reduce both slightly to cook the tartlets properly.

Lancaster lemon tart
20cm (8in) tart

Today we take afternoon tea at 4 or 5 o'clock but in the early days of tea drinking in England, tea was served as an after-dinner 'digestif'. When the last morsels of food had been consumed, the company would retire to a drawing room where the tea table had been prepared.

*175g (6oz) shortcrust pastry
(see page 15)*
150–175g (5–6oz) lemon curd
100g (4oz) butter, softened
100g (4oz) caster sugar
2 large free-range eggs, beaten
3 teaspoons lemon juice
75g (3oz) self-raising flour
25g (1oz) ground almonds
Icing sugar, sifted, for dusting

1 Make the pastry according to the instructions on page 15 and chill for at least 15 minutes.

2 Preheat the oven to 180°C, 350°F, gas mark 4. Grease a 20cm (8in) loose-bottomed round flan dish.

3 On a lightly floured surface, roll out the pastry and use to line the dish. Spread the lemon curd over the base.

4 Beat together the butter and sugar until light and fluffy. Gradually add the beaten eggs and the lemon juice and beat well. Add the flour and ground almonds and fold in with a metal spoon. Spread the batter over the lemon curd and smooth out. Bake for 35 minutes, then reduce the oven temperature to 150°C, 300°F, gas mark 2 and bake for 10–15 minutes more until the sponge is golden and springs back when lightly pressed.

5 Remove from the oven and leave to cool in the dish. When cold, cut into pieces and serve dusted with icing sugar.

Norfolk tart

18cm (7in) tart

Norfolk is more famous for its use of honey in desserts and cakes than for syrup, but this syrup and cream-based recipe makes a delicious teatime treat.

175g (6oz) rich shortcrust pastry
(see page 15)
100g (4oz) golden syrup
1 tablespoon butter
Grated zest of ½ unwaxed lemon
2 tablespoons double cream
1 large free-range egg

1 Make the pastry according to the instructions on page 15 and chill for at least 15 minutes.

2 Preheat the oven to 200°C, 400°F, gas mark 6. Grease an 18cm (7in) round flan dish.

3 On a lightly floured surface, roll out the pastry to make a circle and use to line the prepared dish. Bake blind (see step 3 page 56) for 15–20 minutes. Remove from the oven and lift out the baking beans and paper. Reduce the oven temperature to 180°C, 350°F, gas mark 4.

4 Warm the syrup in a pan with the butter and lemon zest until the butter has dissolved. Beat the cream and egg together and add to the mixture. Pour into the pastry case and bake for 20 minutes until golden and firm. Remove from the oven and serve warm or cold.

Lakeland coconut tart

20cm (8in) tart

This recipe comes from Quarry Bank Mill in Cheshire which thrived as a result of the burgeoning cotton industry of the 18th century. The staple diet of an average worker was potatoes and wheaten bread, washed down with tea or coffee. The Comte de la Rochefoucauld, while touring in England in 1784, wrote, 'Throughout the whole of England the drinking of tea is general. You have it twice a day and though the expense is considerable, the humblest peasant has his tea twice a day just like the rich man'.

175g (6oz) shortcrust pastry
(see page 15)
3–4 tablespoons strawberry or
raspberry jam
100g (4oz) butter
50g (2oz) caster sugar
2 tablespoons golden syrup
225g (8oz) desiccated coconut
2 large free-range eggs, beaten

1 Make the pastry according to the instructions on page 15 and chill for at least 15 minutes.

2 Preheat the oven to 190°C, 375°F, gas mark 5. Grease a 20cm (8in) round flan dish or a deep pie plate.

3 On a lightly floured surface, roll out the pastry and use to line the prepared dish. Spread the jam over the pastry base.

4 Melt together the butter, sugar and syrup and stir in the coconut and beaten eggs. Turn into the pastry case and bake in the centre of the oven for 30 minutes until golden, covering with foil after the first 10 minutes of baking time. Remove from the oven and leave to cool in the dish.

Manchester tart

20cm (8in) tart

This meringue-topped tart is a little like a Queen of Puddings in a pastry shell. The recipe comes from Dunham Massey in Cheshire where the 'tearoom' in the house holds rare tea and coffee tables, the family silver teawares and two tall tea caddies inlaid with mother of pearl. These large tins would have held the main supply of loose-leaf tea and smaller caddies, now on show on side tables and mantel shelves in the drawing and dining rooms, and would have been regularly replenished.

175g (6oz) flaky pastry (see page 14)
3–4 tablespoons raspberry or strawberry jam
Zest of 1 lemon, cut into strips
300ml (10fl oz) milk
50g (2oz) fresh breadcrumbs
50g (2oz) butter, softened
2 large free-range eggs, separated
75g (3oz) caster sugar
1 tablespoon brandy
Caster sugar for dredging

1 Make the pastry according to the instructions on page 14 and chill for at least 45 minutes.

2 Preheat the oven to 190°C, 375°F, gas mark 5. Grease and line a 20cm (8in) round pie dish or loose-bottomed round flan tin.

3 On a floured surface, roll out the pastry and use to line the dish. Spread the jam over the base.

4 Put the lemon zest and milk into a pan and bring to the boil. Strain onto the breadcrumbs and leave for 5 minutes. Add the butter, egg yolks, 2 tablespoons of the sugar and the brandy and beat well. Pour into the pastry case and bake for 45 minutes.

5 Whisk the egg whites until stiff and fold in the remaining sugar. Remove the tart from the oven and spread the meringue over the filling. Dredge with caster sugar and bake for 15 minutes until the meringue is brown.

6 Remove from the oven and leave to cool in the tin. Serve with cream.

Scones &
Slices

Florentine Slice

This chocolate slice is made to a recipe originally from Kingston Lacy in Dorset, once the home of the Bankes family. Margaret Bankes began buying teaware for the house between 1701 and 1710, and acquired various 'setts of tea dishes and saucers', 'a kenester', 'a china sugar dish', a pair of tea tongs, 10 teapots, four tables and 'a black Japan table for my closet', where she took tea.

350g (12oz) good-quality milk or
   plain chocolate
350g (12oz) mixed dried fruit (raisins,
   sultanas, currants, peel)
100g (4oz) glacé cherries
100g (4oz) desiccated coconut
100g (4oz) caster sugar
50g (2oz) butter, melted
2 large free-range eggs, beaten

1   Line a 20 × 27.5cm (8 x 11in) baking tin with foil. Melt the chocolate and spread evenly in the base of the prepared tin. Leave to cool in the fridge until set.

2   Preheat the oven to 180°C, 350°F, gas mark 4.

3   Mix together the dried fruit, glacé cherries, coconut, sugar, butter and beaten eggs, and spread evenly over the chocolate. Bake for 25 minutes until golden brown.

4   Remove from the oven and leave to cool in the tin. When cool, place the tin in the fridge until really cold. Cut into fingers and turn out of the tin.

This rich, gooey slice contains no flour, so is ideal for people who cannot eat wheat.

Apricot Sesame Slice

As well as adding their distinctive flavour and aroma to foods, sesame seeds are rich in minerals and vitamins and also have antioxidant properties. They marry very well with the apricots in this recipe to make a rich and unusual addition to the tea table.

For the base
100g (4oz) butter
100g (4oz) golden syrup
100g (4oz) demerara sugar
225g (8oz) porridge oats
100g (4oz) shredded coconut
50g (2oz) sesame seeds, untoasted
3 teaspoons ground cinnamon
A pinch of salt
100g (4oz) dried apricots, roughly
    chopped
100g (4oz) chocolate chips
    (milk or plain)

For the topping
25g (1oz) sesame seeds, untoasted

1   Preheat the oven to 150°C, 300°F, gas mark 2. Grease a 20 × 27.5cm (8 x 11in) baking tin.

2   Melt the butter and syrup together in a large pan. Add the sugar, oats, coconut, sesame seeds, cinnamon, salt and apricots and stir well, making sure that all the base ingredients are evenly distributed. Stir in the chocolate chips and mix thoroughly.

3   Turn the mixture into the prepared tin, press down firmly and smooth the top. Sprinkle with the sesame seeds and press them well into the mixture. Bake for 30–35 minutes until golden and firm.

4   Remove from the oven and leave to cool in the tin. When cold, cut into slices or squares.

Sweetmince Squares

This Irish recipe includes cinnamon and ginger in the filling. Under Portuguese and then Dutch rule, the island of Sri Lanka was once the world's main producer of cinnamon. Ginger has many health benefits. It is said to help ease nausea, reduce inflammation, settle the digestion, and minimise pain from arthritis. Both spices are also commonly used as additional flavourings for tea.

675g (1lb 8 oz) rich shortcrust
   pastry (see page 15)
1½ teaspoons cornflour
½ teaspoon custard powder
175ml (6fl oz) water
175g (6oz) mixed currants
   and raisins
50g (2oz) chopped mixed peel
75g (3oz) caster, granulated or
   demerara sugar
1 teaspoon ground cinnamon
1 teaspoon mixed spice
½ teaspoon ground ginger
A little water or milk
Caster sugar for dredging

1   Make the pastry according to the instructions on page 15 and chill for at least 15 minutes. Preheat the oven to 180°C, 350°F, gas mark 4. Grease a 18 × 27.5cm (7 x 11in) Swiss roll tin.

2   On a lightly floured surface, roll out half the pastry and use it to line the prepared tin.

3   Mix together the cornflour and custard powder with the water and put in a pan with the water, currants and raisins, mixed peel, granulated sugar, cinnamon, mixed spice and ginger. Bring to the boil and simmer until thick.

4   Gently tip the sweetmince mixture into the pastry case and spread evenly with the back of a spoon.

5   Roll out the remaining pastry and lay it on top. Dampen the edges of the pastry with a little water or milk and press together well. Bake for 45–50 minutes until golden.

6   Remove from the oven and dredge with caster sugar. Allow to cool in the tin. When cold, cut into squares and serve.

Ginger & Treacle Scones

To ensure their supply of quality tea during rationing after World War II, the Bambridge family, from Wimpole Hall in Cambridgeshire, entrusted its stock of tea coupons to Twinings tea company, who delivered the tea in 6kg and 2kg packs. The tea caddies displayed at the house were regularly filled from a large lockable storage bin in the housekeeper's dry basement store.

225g (8oz) self-raising flour
1½ teaspoons baking powder
2 teaspoons ground ginger
50g (2oz) butter, softened and
    cut into small pieces
6 tablespoons milk
1 rounded tablespoon black treacle
A little milk for glazing

1   Preheat the oven to 220°C, 425°F, gas mark 7. Grease a baking sheet.

2   Mix together the flour, baking powder and ginger and rub in the fat until the mixture resembles breadcrumbs.

3   Warm the milk and black treacle together in a small pan until lukewarm. Add to the mixture and mix with a round-bladed knife to a soft dough.

4   On a lightly floured surface, knead the dough until smooth, then roll out to a thickness of 1cm (½in). Cut into circles using a 5cm (2in) cutter and place on the prepared baking sheet.

5   Brush the tops with a little milk. Bake just above the centre of the oven for 10–15 minutes until well risen and golden brown.

6   Remove from the oven and transfer to a wire rack to cool. Serve warm or cold with butter.

Cherry & Almond Scones

Although it was built in the early 15th century, long before the English learnt about tea, Rufford Old Hall in Lancashire has many interesting tea-related items including various unusual teapots and a large ornate 'teapoy' – both a tea table and a storage box – the name deriving from Hindi tipai meaning 'three-footed', since its sturdy leg usually ended in three carved feet.

450g (1lb) self-raising flour
½ teaspoon baking powder
100g (4oz) butter, softened
75g (3oz) caster sugar
175 (3oz) glacé cherries,
   roughly chopped
1 large free-range egg, beaten
A few drops of almond extract
175–200ml (6–7fl oz) milk

1   Preheat the oven to 180°C, 350°F, gas mark 4. Grease two baking sheets.

2   Mix together the flour and baking powder and rub in the butter. Add the sugar, cherries, beaten egg, almond extract and enough milk to give a soft but not sticky dough. Knead lightly until smooth.

3   On a lightly floured surface, roll out to a thickness of 1cm (½in) and cut out circles using a 5cm (2in) cutter. Place on the prepared baking sheets and bake for 20–25 minutes until well risen, firm and golden.

4   Remove from the oven and transfer to a wire rack to cool. Serve with butter or clotted cream and jam.

A delicious variation on the classic scone recipe, glacé cherries and almond extract are a match made in heaven.

Super Scones!

Delicious served with a large dollop of clotted cream and tangy strawberry jam or slathered with butter, these scone recipes are guaranteed to get your mouth watering and your tastebuds tingling!

Eggless scones
12 scones

The name for scones seems to descend from Dutch schoonbrot or German sconbrot meaning 'fine bread', and they appear to have become part of afternoon tea menus in the latter half of the 19th century.

50g (2oz) butter, softened
50g (2oz) lard or vegetable shortening, softened
350g (12oz) self-raising flour
115–125ml (4–4½fl oz) milk

1 Preheat the oven to 190°C, 375°F, gas mark 5. Grease two baking sheets.

2 Rub the butter and lard into the flour, working as quickly and lightly as possible with cold hands. Add enough milk to give a soft, bread-like dough.

3 On a lightly floured surface, roll out to a thickness of 1.5cm (¾in) and cut into circles with a 6cm (2½in) cutter. Place on the prepared baking sheets and bake for 15–20 minutes until lightly golden and well risen.

4 Remove from the oven and transfer to a wire rack to cool. These plain, light, well-risen scones are perfect served warm with jam and Cornish clotted cream.

Cheese scones

12 scones

Savoury scones make a satisfying part of high tea. This version is delicious served warm from the oven with a bowl of hot soup.

450g (1lb) self-raising flour
115g (4oz) soft margarine
140g (5oz) grated mature
  Cheddar cheese
Salt and ground black pepper
1 egg
150ml (5fl oz) milk
1 teaspoon English mustard

1 Preheat the oven to 200°C, 400°F, gas mark 4. Grease a baking sheet.

2 Mix together the flour and salt and pepper and rub in the margarine until you have fine breadcrumbs. Add all but 25g of the cheese. Stir together the egg, 125ml of milk and the mustard and add to the flour mixture. Mix to make a smooth, soft dough.

3 On a floured surface, lightly knead the dough then cut in half. Shape each half into a ball, roll out slightly then cut each circle into quarters. Place on the baking sheet, brush the tops with the remaining milk and sprinkle with the cheese. Bake for 10–15 minutes until golden.

Making one large scone disc instead of small individual ones is possible with all types of scone dough, as long as you make the dough an even thickness.

Fruit scones
8 scones

The ultimate English treat, these scones are best served simply with good strawberry jam and generous spoonfuls of clotted cream.

450g (1lb) self-raising flour
115g (4oz) soft margarine
85g (3oz) caster sugar
85g (3oz) sultanas
1 large egg
200ml (7fl oz) milk

1 Preheat the oven to 200°C, 400°F, gas mark 7. Grease two baking sheets.

2 Mix together the flour, salt and baking powder and rub in the butter. Stir in the sugar and sultanas then add the egg. Gradually mix in two thirds of the milk to make a soft dough.

3 On a lightly floured surface, roll out to a thickness of 2cm (¾in) and cut into circles using a 7cm (2¾in) cutter. Place on the prepared baking sheets, brush with milk and bake for 10–15 minutes until golden.

4 Remove from the oven and transfer to a wire rack to cool. Serve warm or cold.

All kinds of dried fruit can be incorporated successfully into scones. Try cranberries with a little grated orange or lime zest, or you could go for a tropical feel with mango, papaya and pineapple.

Irish honey scones

18cm (7in) scone round

Should clotted cream go on the scone before or after the jam? It depends on where the scone is being eaten. In Devon, cream goes first because it is possible to get more cream to stay on the scone! In Cornwall, jam goes first. Which way is 'correct' is a debate that has been raging for centuries between the two counties.

100g (4oz) plain wholemeal flour
100g (4oz) plain white flour
2 teaspoons baking powder
A pinch of salt
75g (3oz) butter, softened
1 tablespoon light soft brown sugar
2 tablespoons clear honey
50–75ml (2–3fl oz) milk

1 Preheat the oven to 200°C, 400°F, gas mark 6. Grease a baking sheet.

2 Mix together the flours, baking powder and salt and rub in the butter. Add the sugar and mix. Mix the honey with the milk and stir until the honey has dissolved. Reserve a little for glazing and add the rest to the flour. Mix to a soft dough.

3 Place the dough on the prepared sheet and shape with the hands into a flat circle approximately 18cm (7in) in diameter. Divide the top into eight wedges. Bake for 15–20 minutes until risen.

4 Remove from the oven, glaze the top with the honey and milk mixture and return to the oven for a further 5–10 minutes until golden. Remove from the oven and serve warm with jam and cream or butter.

Clotted cream is a thick cream made by heating full-fat cow's milk indirectly, using a water bath or steam, and then leaving it in shallow pans to cool slowly and form 'clots'.

Teabreads & *Loaves*

Herb Bread

450g
(1lb)
loaf

This herby, cheesy bread is full of flavour. You can vary the herbs you use to match what you have growing in your garden, what you are serving it with, or what kind of cheese you want to use. Equally, you can alter the type of cheese to suit your taste – as long as it has plenty of flavour it's sure to be delicious served with some cold, fresh butter.

225g (8oz) self-raising flour (white or a mixture of half white and half wholemeal)
1 teaspoon dry English mustard powder
2 tablespoons fresh chopped herbs (chives, thyme, basil, sage, parsley)
100g (4oz) mature Cheddar cheese, grated
25g (1oz) butter
1 large free-range egg, beaten
150ml (5fl oz) water

1 Preheat the oven to 190°C, 375°F, gas mark 5. Grease a 450g (1lb) loaf tin.

2 Mix together the flour, mustard, herbs and cheese. Melt the butter, add to the mixture with the egg and water and mix until it forms a soft, wet, cake-like dough.

3 Turn into the prepared tin and bake for 45 minutes until well risen and golden brown. Remove from the oven and cool on a wire rack. Serve warm or cold with butter.

Serve it as the savoury element to afternoon tea in thin slices spread with butter, or pack it as part of a delicious summer picnic.

Date & Walnut Loaf

900g (2lb) loaf

This typical Cornish recipe uses spices, brown sugar and exotic fruit. From the 17th century, ships from the Orient imported such luxuries through the Cornish ports and these were included in many cake recipes. The immense oven in the north wall of the kitchen has almost certainly baked a number of these loaves over the centuries.

225g (8oz) self-raising flour
50g (2oz) walnut halves
1 teaspoon mixed spice
75g (3oz) butter
100g (4oz) light or dark soft
    brown sugar
225g (8oz) whole dates
150ml (5fl oz) water
2 large free-range eggs, beaten
2 tablespoons sesame seeds

1 Preheat the oven to 180°C, 350°F, gas mark 4. Grease and line a 900g (2lb) loaf tin.

2 Mix together the flour, walnuts and mixed spice.

3 Place the butter, sugar, dates and water in a pan and bring gently to the boil. Remove from the heat and cool for a few minutes. Add to the flour, spice and nuts with the beaten eggs and beat well.

4 Turn into the prepared tin, hollow the centre a little and sprinkle the top with the sesame seeds. Bake for 1–1¼ hours until a skewer inserted in the centre comes out clean.

5 Remove from the oven and turn out onto a wire rack to cool. Serve sliced with butter.

Blackberry Teabread

900g (2lb) loaf

Made with freshly harvested hedgerow berries, this tea loaf, originally from Trelissick in Cornwall makes a delicious change from traditional fruited breads. The garden here was created by Ronald Copeland who was managing director of the Spode china factory. Many flowers that flourish in the mild Cornish air were the inspiration for the floral designs produced at the works.

350g (12oz) plain flour
1 teaspoon mixed spice
175g (6oz) butter, softened
175g (6oz) caster sugar
225g (8oz) fresh or frozen
    blackberries (if frozen, use
    straight from the freezer)
Grated zest and juice of
    1 unwaxed lemon
1 tablespoon black treacle
2 large free-range eggs, beaten
½ teaspoon bicarbonate of soda
2 tablespoons milk

1 Preheat the oven to 180°C, 350°F, gas mark 4. Grease and line a 900g (2lb) loaf tin.

2 Mix together the flour and mixed spice and rub in the butter until the mixture resembles fine breadcrumbs.

3 Add the sugar, blackberries, lemon zest and juice, black treacle and eggs and mix well. Dissolve the bicarbonate of soda in the milk, add to the mixture and beat well.

4 Pour into the prepared tin, smooth the top and bake for 45 minutes. Reduce the oven temperature to 150°C, 300°F, gas mark 2 and cook for a further 30–45 minutes until a skewer inserted in the centre comes out clean.

5 Remove from the oven and leave to cool in the tin for about 15 minutes before turning out onto a wire rack to cool completely.

This unusual loaf is an ideal and novel way of using the blackberries that flourish in British hedgerows every summer.

Barm Brack

900g
(2lb)
loaf

Barm means 'leaven' and brack means 'speckled', as the fruit is scattered through the plain dough. It was often made in flattened circles, and is served sliced, sometimes toasted, with lots of butter. At Hallowe'en, tokens were concealed in the dough to predict the fortune of the recipient – a coin meant riches, a ring foretold a wedding, a stick an unhappy marriage and a pea no marriage at all!

100g (4oz) currants
100g (4oz) sultanas
100g (4oz) raisins
50g (2oz) chopped mixed peel
50g (2oz) glacé cherries, quartered
200g (7oz) light soft brown sugar
300ml (10fl oz) cold black tea
Grated zest of 1 unwaxed lemon
2 large free-range eggs, beaten
250g (9oz) self-raising flour
1 teaspoon mixed spice
A pinch of salt

1 Put the dried fruit and glacé cherries into a bowl with the sugar, tea and lemon zest and leave to soak for at least 3 hours, preferably longer.

2 Preheat the oven to 180°C, 350°F, gas mark 4. Grease and line a 900g (2lb) loaf tin.

3 Add the eggs, flour, mixed spice and salt to the fruit mixture and mix until well combined.

4 Turn into the prepared loaf tin and bake for 1½–1¾ hours until a skewer inserted in the centre comes out clean.

5 Remove from the oven and turn out onto a wire rack to cool. Serve sliced with butter.

Chelsea Buns

London's Chelsea Buns were originally made and sold in the Old Chelsea Bun House, a bakery in Pimlico, London. The owner and manager was a certain Richard Hand, who was known by most people as Captain Bun.

225g (8oz) strong white bread flour
15g (½oz) fresh yeast (to substitute dried yeast, see page 216)
1 teaspoon caster sugar
100ml (4fl oz) warm milk
15g (½oz) lard or shortening, softened
A pinch of salt
1 large free-range egg, beaten
50g (2oz) butter, melted
50g (2oz) raisins
50g (2oz) currants
50g (2oz) sultanas
25g (1oz) chopped mixed peel
50g (2oz) light soft brown sugar
Clear honey for glazing

1 Grease an 18cm (7in) square cake tin. Put 50g (2oz) of the flour into a bowl and add the yeast, caster sugar and milk. Mix to a smooth batter and leave in a warm place for 20 minutes until frothy.

2 Rub the lard or shortening into the remaining flour. Add the salt, the yeast mixture and the beaten egg, and mix to a soft dough. Knead on a lightly floured surface for about 5 minutes until really smooth. Place in a bowl, cover with a clean, damp cloth and leave in a warm place for 1–1½ hours until doubled in size.

3 Knead the dough again on a lightly floured surface and then roll out to a rectangle 23 × 30cm (9 x 12in). Brush the melted butter over the surface and sprinkle the dried fruit and brown sugar over, leaving a narrow border all the way round the edge. Roll up like a Swiss roll, starting with the longer side. Brush the edges of the dough with water and seal.

4 Cut the roll into nine pieces and place the rolls, cut-side uppermost, in the prepared tin. Leave in a warm place for a further 30 minutes until well risen.

5 Meanwhile, preheat the oven to 190°C, 375°F, gas mark 5.

6 When the buns are risen, bake for 30–35 minutes until golden. Remove from the oven, turn out on to a wire rack and, while still warm, brush the tops with honey. To serve, pull apart and eat warm or cold.

Marmalade & Apricot Teabread

450g
(1lb)
loaf

Marmalade is commonly associated with breakfast than teatime, as it is the British favourite for spreading on hunks of warm toast on top of lashings of unsalted butter. This delightful cake brings the familiar tangy flavours of marmalade to the tea table, softened with the addition of soft dried apricots.

200g (7oz) plain flour
2 teaspoons ground ginger
1 teaspoon baking powder
50g (2oz) unsalted butter
50g (2oz) dark brown sugar
100g (4oz) chopped ready-to-eat
    dried apricots
4 tablespoons marmalade
75ml (2½fl oz) milk
1 large free-range egg, beaten

1 Preheat the oven to 160°C, 325°F, gas mark 3. Grease and line a 450g (1lb) loaf tin.

2 Sift the flour, ginger and baking powder into a large bowl and rub in the butter until the mixture looks like breadcrumbs. Then stir in the sugar and the chopped apricots.

3 In another bowl or jug, mix together the marmalade, milk and egg. Pour it onto the dry mixture and mix thoroughly. Pour it into the prepared tin and level the top. Bake for about 1 hour, or until golden, firm to the touch and a skewer inserted in the centre comes out clean.

4 Remove from the oven and turn out onto a wire rack to cool.

5 You can make some candied orange peel to go on top, but this is entirely optional. All you need to do is pare some strips of orange zest and put them into a pan with about 150ml (5fl oz) water and 3 tablespoons caster sugar. Bring to the boil and then slowly simmer for about an hour, or until the zest has become translucent and the liquid has reduced by about half. Be careful not to reduce the liquid to a caramel. Remove the orange strips from the pan and leave on baking paper to cool and dry, then sprinkle with more caster sugar.

Gently Spiced Fruit Loaf

900g
(2lb)
loaf

The brioche-style dough for this rich and fruity loaf is rolled with a sumptuous dried-fruit filling seasoned with cardamom, honey and citrus, and finished with flaked almonds and a generous drizzle of lemon icing. A loaf to grace any tea time table.

For the dough:
40g (1½oz) unsalted butter
275g (9½oz) strong white
    bread flour
50g (2oz) caster sugar
A pinch of salt
7g (¼ oz) sachet fast-action
    dried yeast
100ml (4fl oz) hand-hot milk
3 large free-range egg yolks

For the filling:
500ml (17fl oz) water
450g (1lb) dried fruit (apricots,
    cranberries, dates, figs,
    peaches, etc.), chopped
Zest and juice of 1 large unwaxed
    lemon
Zest and juice of 1 large orange
2 tablespoons clear honey
1 teaspoon ground coriander
1 teaspoon cardamom seeds, crushed

For the icing:
75g (3oz) icing sugar, sifted
Juice of 1 large lemon
Flaked almonds for sprinkling
    (optional)

1   In a large bowl, rub the butter into the flour until it resembles breadcrumbs, then stir in the sugar, salt and yeast. Pour in the hot milk and 2 egg yolks and mix to form a dough. Turn the dough out onto a lightly floured surface and knead for at least 10 minutes until smooth and elastic. Put the dough in the bowl, cover with a tea towel or cling film and leave in a warm place to rise for at least 1 hour until doubled in size.

2   While the dough is rising, make the filling. Bring the water to the boil in a large pan, add the dried fruit and simmer, stirring occasionally, until the fruit is really soft. Add the citrus zest and juice, honey and spices and simmer gently until the liquid has been absorbed, stirring occasionally. Leave the mixture to cool.

3   Knock the air out of the dough and knead it again for another 3–4 minutes. On a lightly floured surface, roll it out into a large rectangle about 1cm (½in) thick. Spread the fruit over the surface,

leaving a 1.5cm (¾in) gap round the edge. Roll up the dough as you would a Swiss roll and press the edges together to seal, then coil it around to make a circular sausage. Place it on a baking sheet with the seal underneath. Cover again and leave to rise for a further 1 hour.

4   Preheat the oven to 180°C, 350°F, gas mark 4.

5   Just before the loaf goes in the oven, brush it all over with the remaining egg yolk. Bake for about 20 minutes until it is risen and golden on the top and sounds hollow when tapped on the base.

6   Remove from the oven and transfer to a wire rack to cool.

7   Put the icing sugar in a small bowl and gradually drip in the lemon juice, blending to a thin icing. When the loaf is cool, randomly drizzle the icing over the top of the loaf and sprinkle the almonds on top, if you like.

Apple & Walnut Teabread

900g (2lb) loaf

This recipe makes one of the most versatile teabreads you can bake, and is especially delicious in the autumn when apples come into season. It will work large or small, sweet or savoury, and tastes superb on any tea table with a piece of strong Cheddar, or equally good with butter and a cup of tea – even packed in a lunch box. It keeps well in an airtight container.

100g (4oz) unsalted butter
100g (4oz) caster sugar
2 large free-range eggs
1 tablespoon golden syrup
100g (4oz) sultanas
100g (4oz) chopped walnuts
225g (8oz) self-raising flour
1 teaspoon mixed spice
1 teaspoon ground cinnamon
2 dessert apples, peeled,
    cored and chopped

1 Preheat the oven to 160°C, 325°F, gas mark 3. Grease and line a 900g (2lb) loaf tin or lay out 12 mini loaf cases on a baking sheet.

2 Put all the ingredients into a large bowl and beat until well mixed, either by hand or in a mixer. For best results, do not use a food processor as it will break down the apple too much.

3 Tip the mixture into the prepared tin or mini loaf cases and bake the large loaf for about 1 hour or the small ones for about 20 minutes, or until a skewer inserted in the centre comes out clean.

4 Turn a large loaf out onto a wire rack to cool, or leave little ones to cool in their cases.

Ultimate Loaf Cakes

Cakes cooked in a loaf tin are a British teatime staple – serve as elegant slices on dainty plates for a sophisticated afternoon tea, with butter on the side for extra indulgence.

Fig & raisin teabread
900g (2lb) loaf

Naturally sweet, soft, yet slightly crunchy from the seeds and really good for you, dried figs are healthy and taste good in baked foods. Here, they make a rich and decadent loaf.

225g (8oz) plain flour
100g (4oz) unsalted butter
100g (4oz) dried figs, chopped
100g (4oz) demerara sugar
50g (2oz) pecan nuts, chopped (optional)
100g (4oz) raisins
1 teaspoon baking powder
1 teaspoon bicarbonate of soda
150ml (5fl oz) milk

1 Preheat the oven to 160°C, 325°F, gas mark 3. Grease and line a 900g (2lb) loaf tin.

2 Put the flour into a large bowl and rub in the butter until the mixture looks like breadcrumbs. Stir in the figs, sugar, pecan nuts, if using, and raisins.

3 Mix together the baking powder, bicarbonate of soda and milk, then pour into the dry mix and blend thoroughly, adding a drop more milk if you need to, so that you have a good dropping consistency. Turn the batter into the prepared tin and bake for 1 hour, or until firm to the touch and a skewer inserted in the centre comes out clean.

4 Remove from the oven and turn out onto a wire rack to cool.

Malt loaf
450g (1lb) loaf

It is said that malt loaf is the ideal snack for breastfeeding women as it is full of energy-giving properties, packed with vitamins, easy to eat one-handed and something of a superfood. It should certainly not be restricted to new mothers, however, as it is delicious sliced and buttered on the tea table or as an anytime snack. Malt extract is available in wholefood stores.

100g (4oz) raisins
100g (4oz) sultanas
100g (4oz) unsalted butter
150ml (5fl oz) water
175g (6oz) self-raising flour
½ teaspoon bicarbonate of soda
A pinch of salt
100g (4oz) soft dark brown sugar
1 large free-range egg, beaten
1 tablespoon malt extract

1 Preheat the oven to 180°C, 350°F, gas mark 4. Grease and line a 450g (1lb) loaf tin.

2 Put the dried fruit, butter and water into a pan and bring to the boil, then reduce the heat and simmer gently for 5 minutes. Leave to cool.

3 In a large bowl, mix together the flour, bicarbonate of soda, salt and sugar. Stir in the fruit mixture followed by the egg and the malt. Stir all the ingredients together well.

4 Turn the batter into the prepared tin and bake for about 1 hour, or until a skewer inserted in the centre comes out clean.

5 Leave to cool in the tin, then turn out and serve sliced and buttered.

Earl Grey loaf
900g (2lb) loaf

If you don't like Earl Grey tea, simply substitute your favourite, such as Assam, Darjeeling, Lapsang Souchong, or even your usual breakfast tea. This recipe is made without any fat, but still has that rich flavour expected of a tea loaf. Serve it sliced and buttered. If possible, start preparations the night before.

225g (8oz) raisins or sultanas
175ml (6fl oz) strong cold Earl Grey tea
225g (8oz) self-raising flour
175g (6oz) demerara sugar
1 large free-range egg

1 Soak the raisins in the tea overnight, if possible.

2 The next day, preheat the oven to 160°C, 325°F, gas mark 3 and grease and line a 900g (2lb) loaf tin.

3 If you haven't been organized enough to soak your fruit, put the raisins and the tea in a pan and bring to the boil, then reduce the heat and simmer gently for 20 minutes. The results will not be quite as good but will still make a good loaf.

4 Tip the fruit and remaining tea into a large bowl and stir in all the other ingredients. Turn the batter into the prepared tin and bake for about 1 hour, or until a skewer inserted in the centre comes out clean. Leave to cool in the tin for 10 minutes before turning out onto a wire rack to cool completely.

Simone Sekers's Fruit Parkin
16 squares

Parkin is nutty gingerbread made with oatmeal instead of flour. Traditionally a Hallowe'en speciality, parkins probably derive from the pagan practice of baking oatmeal and spice cakes for celebrations to mark the start of winter. In Derbyshire they were named after Thor, the Scandinavian god of thunder, war and agriculture. They were sometimes called 'tharve' or hearth cakes, as they were cooked on a bakestone in the open fire.

400ml (15fl oz) water
100g (4oz) lard
195g (6oz) light or dark soft brown sugar
225g (8oz) golden syrup
225g (8oz) black treacle
100g (4oz) currants
50g (2oz) chopped mixed peel
450g (1lb) plain flour
225g (8oz) medium oatmeal
2 teaspoons mixed spice
1½ teaspoons ground ginger
A pinch of salt
1 teaspoon bicarbonate of soda dissolved in a little water

1 Preheat the oven to 160°C, 325°F, gas mark 3. Grease and line a 20 × 30cm (8 × 12in) roasting tin.

2 Gently heat the water, lard, sugar syrup and treacle in a pan until melted. Leave to cool slightly. Add all the remaining ingredients and mix together thoroughly.

3 Turn into the prepared tin and bake for 1–1½ hours until firm and well risen.

4 Remove from the oven and leave to cool in the tin before turning out onto a wire rack to cool completely. Cut into squares to serve.

Date & walnut teabread
900g (2lb) loaf

Dates have a natural affinity with teabreads. Their sweetness and moistness adds not just flavour but the gorgeous texture that is called for here. Dates and walnuts, of course, are no strangers in cooking, and they make a perfect combination in this teabread.

100g (4oz) unsalted butter
3 tablespoons golden syrup
1 tablespoon black treacle
150ml (5fl oz) milk
2 large free-range eggs
150g (9oz) wholemeal plain flour
1 teaspoon ground cinnamon
1 teaspoon bicarbonate of soda
75g (3oz) chopped walnuts
225g (8oz) stoned dates, chopped

1 Preheat the oven to 160°C, 325°F, gas mark 3. Grease and line a 900g (2lb) loaf tin.

2 Melt the butter, syrup and treacle together in a pan over a low heat. Remove from the heat and stir in the milk, then leave to cool a little. Beat in the eggs (they will scramble if you add them too soon).

3 Sift the dry ingredients into a large bowl, then beat in the syrup mixture and fold in the walnuts and dates. Turn the batter into the prepared tin and bake for about 1½ hours until a skewer inserted in the centre comes out clean.

4 Remove from the oven and leave to cool in the tin.

Lavender teabread
680g (1½lb) loaf

Lavender may sound odd in a cake to modern ears but it is actually very traditional. This teabread is one for a summer tea, and goes well spread generously with mascarpone cheese and topped with some fresh, juicy strawberries.

3 tablespoons lavender flowers
180ml (6fl oz) milk
175g (6oz) unsalted butter
175g (6oz) caster sugar
2 large free-range eggs, beaten
350g (12oz) plain flour
A pinch of salt
1 teaspoon baking powder

1 Preheat the oven to 325°F, gas mark 3. Grease and line a 900g (2lb) loaf tin.

2 Put the lavender flowers in a small pan with the milk. Gently heat the milk until it barely reaches a simmer, then remove from the heat and let the lavender infuse in the milk for 20 minutes or so.

3 In a large bowl, cream the butter and sugar until light and fluffy, then gradually beat in the eggs. Sift half the flour over the mixture together with the salt and baking powder and fold this in. Then carefully fold in half the milk and lavender mixture. Follow this with the second half of the flour and, finally, the remaining milk.

4 Turn the batter into the prepared tin and bake for about 50 minutes, or until a skewer inserted in the centre comes out clean.

5 Remove from the oven and leave to cool in the tin for about 10 minutes before turning out onto a wire rack to cool completely.

If you can't find lavender, this recipe also works well with other fragrant herbs such as rosemary or lemon balm. Make sure the herbs haven't been sprayed with any chemicals and wash them well before you use them.

Lardy cake

8 slices

This may well be the most unhealthy, artery-clogging cake you will ever come across. It is also part of Britain's heritage and has been around for so many years simply because it is so amazingly delicious. It is filling, sweet, doughy, chewy and comforting.

25g (1oz) fresh yeast (to substitute dried yeast see page 216)
300ml (10fl oz) warm water
1 teaspoon caster sugar
450g (1lb) strong white bread flour
2 teaspoons salt
175g (6oz) lard or vegetable shortening, chilled
75g (3oz) currants
75g (3oz) sultanas
75g (3oz) raisins
175g (6oz) caster sugar

1 Grease and line a 20 × 25cm (8 x 10in) baking tin.

2 Crumble the yeast over the warm water and add 1 teaspoon sugar. Blend until the yeast dissolves, then set aside for 15 minutes.

3 Put the flour and salt into a large bowl and add 1 tablespoon of the lard. Rub the lard into the flour and then add the yeast liquid and mix to a dough.

4 Turn the dough out onto a lightly floured surface and knead for about 10 minutes, or until it is smooth and elastic. Put the dough back in the bowl, cover with cling film and leave in a warm place for 30 minutes to rise.

5 Take the dough out of the bowl, knock out the air and roll it into a rectangle about 5mm (¼in) thick. Cut the remaining lard into little cubes and sprinkle a third of it over the dough, followed by a third of the fruit and a third of the sugar.

6 Fold the bottom third of the dough upwards and the top third of the dough downwards and give the whole thing a half turn so that you have a vertical rectangle in front of you. Roll this out until you get back to a 5mm (¼in) thick rectangle, then repeat the process twice more until you have incorporated all the fat, sugar and fruit. Roll out the dough to fit the prepared tin and carefully lift it into the tin. Stab it 6–8 times right the way through the dough. Cover with a tea towel and leave to rise in a warm place for 30 minutes.

7 Preheat the oven to 220°C, 425°F, gas mark 7.

8 Score the top of the cake into 8, if you like, and bake for about 45 minutes, or until golden brown.

9 Remove from the oven and leave to cool in the tin. If it sticks when you try to turn it out, heat it gently, remove from the tin and spread the contents of the tin back over the cake.

Bara brith
10 slices

This is a traditional Welsh teabread, similar to Barm Brack, both names meaning 'speckled bread'. There are many versions of this delicious loaf – some use yeast, others self-raising flour. This version, made with self-raising flour, is simplicity itself and really calls for plenty of butter. You can make it with cold tea instead of the wine, if you prefer.

350g (12oz) mixed dried fruit
350ml (12fl oz) red wine
100g (4oz) butter
100g (4oz) light soft brown sugar
50ml (2fl oz) milk
1 tablespoon black treacle
225g (8oz) self-raising flour
1 teaspoon mixed spice
2 large free-range eggs, beaten

1 Soak the fruit overnight in the red wine. The next day, preheat the oven to 180°C, 350°F, gas mark 4 and grease and line a 900g (2lb) loaf tin.

2 Add the butter, sugar, milk and treacle to the fruit, bring to the boil and simmer for 5 minutes. Remove from the heat and leave to cool. Add the flour, mixed spice and beaten eggs and mix well.

3 Turn into the prepared tin and bake just below the centre of the oven for about 1½ hours until a skewer inserted in the centre comes out clean.

4 Transfer to a wire rack to cool completely before slicing and serving spread with butter.

Bite-sized
Treats

English Madeleines

These fun little cakes couldn't be more different from their better-known and more sophisticated French counterparts, and are ideal when you want something a little more light-hearted and fun on your tea table. They are usually baked in a traditional dariole mould but they are delightful in these little pudding basins.

100g (4oz) unsalted butter
100g (4oz) caster sugar
2 large free-range eggs, lightly
  beaten
100g (4oz) self-raising flour
3 tablespoons strawberry jam, sieved
75g (3oz) desiccated coconut
8 glacé cherries

1 Preheat the oven to 160°C, 325°F, gas mark 3 and grease your chosen moulds. You might like to line the base with a disc of baking parchment too, just to be on the safe side.

2 Beat the butter and the sugar together until really light and fluffy, then gradually beat in the eggs, a little at a time. Then fold in the flour. Spoon the batter into the prepared moulds and bake for about 20 minutes, until springy and firm to the touch.

3 Remove from the oven and leave to cool in their moulds for 5 minutes before turning them out onto a wire rack to cool completely. If they stick in the moulds, run a knife along the edge of the moulds and give them a good sharp tap on the bottom.

4 When the cakes are completely cold, slice off the tops so that they have a very flat base when you turn them upside-down. Brush the jam over the whole of each cake. Put the coconut in a shallow plate. Insert a skewer in the base of one cake and roll it in the coconut until covered. Repeat with the remaining cakes, then top each one with a glacé cherry.

Macaroons

20 cakes

Macaroons bring a modern and colourful touch to a tea table, and offer a welcome variety with their crisp outside layer and squidgy insides. If you make them neat and small, you can also enjoy quite a few without looking too greedy. This is the basic version, so you can add your favourite flavours. You can make them with rosewater, lavender, lime, mandarin, lemon or bergamot.

175g (6oz) icing sugar
125g (4½oz) ground almonds
3 large free-range egg whites
75g (3oz) caster sugar
Food colouring (optional)
2–3 drops of flavouring (optional)
75g (3oz) unsalted butter, softened
150g (5oz) icing sugar, sifted

1   Preheat the oven to 160°C, 325°F, gas mark 3 and line two baking sheets with baking parchment.

2   In a food processor, blitz the icing sugar and ground almonds so that they are very fine, then sift the mixture into a large bowl. Discard any chunky bits that remain in the sieve.

3   In another bowl, whisk the egg whites until stiff and then whisk in the caster sugar until you have a glossy meringue. Add the food colouring and the flavouring to the meringue and continue to whisk.

4   Very carefully, fold the meringue into the dry ingredients and continue folding until the mixture leaves a ribbon trail. Carefully spoon the mixture into a decorating bag fitted with a plain tube and pipe small shapes about 2.5cm (1in) across onto the prepared baking sheets, leaving a good gap between each macaroon.

5   Now leave the macaroons to dry out in the air until they form a skin. Do not attempt to bake them while they are tacky to the touch. This may take 10–45 minutes, depending on the humidity of the surroundings.

6   Put the macaroons in the oven for 15 minutes to dry. If you gently nudge them along the liner and they don't move, give them another 2 minutes. When ready, remove from the oven and transfer to a wire rack to cool.

7   Make the buttercream filling by beating the butter and the icing sugar together. Add colour and flavour to match the macaroons and, when they are cool, sandwich them together and pile them onto serving plates.

Eccles Cakes

These fruity cakes – the puff pastry delights from the town of the same name – are traditionally made with chopped mixed peel, but if you aren't keen on the flavour you can make your Eccles cakes with just currants, as the recipe below suggests. If you are a fan of mixed peel, try adding a tablespoon to the currant mixture for a more traditional version.

225–80g (8–10oz) flaky pastry
(see page 14)
25g (1oz) butter, softened
25g (1oz) light soft brown sugar
75g (3oz) currants
1 teaspoon mixed spice
A little milk or water
1 large free-range egg white, beaten
2 tablespoons caster sugar

1   Make the pastry according to the instructions on page 14, then chill for 1 hour.

2   Preheat the oven to 220°C, 425°F, gas mark 7 and grease two baking sheets.

3   Roll out the pastry to about 5mm (¼in) thick and cut out about 10 circles using a 10cm (4in) cutter.

4   In a bowl, mix together the butter, sugar, currants and mixed spice. Place a teaspoon of the mixture into the centre of each pastry circle. Dampen the edges of the pastry with a little milk or water, bundle up the outer edges as if to make a purse and squidge the edges together to seal.

5   Turn each parcel over, sealed-side down, and roll it out into a flatter circle so that the currants just start to peek through. Prick all over with a fork and place on the prepared baking sheets. Brush with beaten egg and bake for about 15 minutes, until golden brown.

6   Remove from the oven and transfer to a wire rack to cool. Sprinkle with caster sugar while they are still warm.

Apple Muffins with Cinnamon Butter

So easy and so comforting, these muffins will fill your kitchen with the sweet smell of cinnamon while they bake. For a really special finish, serve them still warm, broken open and spread with melting cinnamon butter.

300g (10oz) self-raising flour
½ teaspoon bicarbonate of soda
1 teaspoon ground cinnamon
2 large free-range eggs, beaten
75ml (3fl oz) plain yogurt
100ml (4fl oz) milk
100g (4oz) soft brown sugar
6 tablespoons sunflower oil
2 apples, peeled, cored and
    finely diced

For the cinnamon butter
100g (4oz) butter, at room
    temperature
75g (3oz) icing sugar, sifted
1 teaspoon ground cinnamon

1   Preheat the oven to 200°F, 400°F, gas mark 6. Grease or line a 12-hole muffin tin.

2   Combine the flour, bicarbonate of soda and cinnamon and sift into a large bowl.

3   In a separate bowl, combine the eggs, yogurt, milk, brown sugar and oil, then stir in the apples. Pour the mixture into the dry ingredients and stir together until just combined, then spoon the batter into the prepared muffin tin.

4   Bake for about 20 minutes until risen and golden. Leave to cool in the tin for a couple of minutes, before turning out onto a wire rack to cool.

5   Meanwhile, beat together the butter, icing sugar and cinnamon. Serve the muffins warm, with the cinnamon butter for spreading.

Lemon & Almond Crumbles

12 muffins

Lemon and almond flavours permeate these moist and moreish cakes, which somehow elicit an air of sophistication and make you feel rather ladylike – even though they are so simple and quick to make and serve.

225g (8oz) self-raising flour
1 teaspoon baking powder
150g (5oz) caster sugar
100g (4oz) ground almonds
1 large free-range egg, beaten
225ml (8fl oz) milk
75g (3oz) butter, melted
Grated zest of 2 lemons
50g (2oz) flaked almonds for
    sprinkling
Icing sugar for dusting

1 Preheat the oven to 200°F, 400°F, gas mark 6. Grease or line a 12-hole muffin tin.

2 Combine the flour, baking powder and caster sugar and sift into a large bowl. Sprinkle the ground almonds into the bowl.

3 In a separate bowl or jug, combine the egg, milk, butter and lemon zest, then pour into the dry ingredients. Stir together until just combined, then place large spoonfuls of the batter into the prepared muffin tin. Sprinkle the tops with the flaked almonds.

4 Bake for about 20 minutes until risen and golden. Leave to cool in the tin for a few minutes, then transfer to a wire rack to cool completely. Serve dusted with icing sugar.

These dainty muffins are even cuter if you make them in a mini muffin tin — but be sure to reduce the baking time slightly.

Espresso Express

Make these in the morning when you need a bit of a lift to get you going. After munching your way through the coffee-flavoured crumb, specked with whole chocolate-covered coffee beans and topped with a lusciously creamy, sugary coffee buttercream, nothing is going to stop you!

200g (7oz) plain flour
1 tablespoon baking powder
150g (5oz) caster sugar
40g (1½oz) chocolate-covered
   coffee beans
1 large free-range egg, beaten
175ml (6fl oz) milk
2 tablespoons Greek yogurt
2 tablespoons instant coffee,
   dissolved in 2 tablespoons boiling
   water
75g (3oz) butter, melted

For the topping
100g (4oz) butter, at room
   temperature
200g (7oz) icing sugar, sifted
2 teaspoons instant coffee, dissolved
   in 1 tablespoon boiling water
Chocolate-covered coffee beans to
   decorate

1 Preheat the oven to 200°F, 400°F, gas mark 6. Grease or line a 12-hole muffin tin.

2 Combine the flour, baking powder and caster sugar and sift into a large bowl, then scatter the coffee beans on top.

3 In a separate bowl or jug, lightly beat together the egg, milk, yogurt and coffee, then stir in the melted butter. Pour into the dry ingredients and stir together until just combined, then spoon into the prepared tin.

4 Bake for about 20 minutes until risen and firm to the touch. Leave to cool in the tin for a few minutes, then transfer the muffins to a wire rack to cool completely.

5 To decorate, beat together the butter, icing sugar and coffee until smooth and creamy. Swirl on top of the muffins and decorate with more chocolate-covered coffee beans.

Peppermint Stick Muffins

Let the children help you make these magnificently minty muffins – they'll love bashing the mints to break them up. Look out for stripy sticks of rock or candy cane and tint the icing in a contrasting colour or bake them in novelty muffin tins to really make them stand out.

300g (10oz) self-raising flour
1 teaspoon baking powder
75g (3oz) caster sugar
2 × 40g (1½oz) packets of extra
    strong mints
2 large free-range eggs, beaten
225ml (8fl oz) milk
75g (3oz) butter, melted

To decorate
3 × 75g (3oz) sticks of peppermint
    candy cane or rock
200g (7oz) icing sugar, sifted
2 tablespoons lemon juice
Food colouring (optional)
Candy cane or rock, to decorate

1   Preheat the oven to 200°F, 400°F, gas mark 6. Grease and line a 12-hole muffin tin or individual muffin moulds.

2   Combine the flour, baking powder and caster sugar, then sift into a bowl. Put the mints in a mortar and pound with a pestle to break them up into small pieces. Scatter them over the flour.

3   In a separate bowl or jug, lightly beat together the eggs and milk to combine, then stir in the butter. Pour into the dry ingredients and stir together until just combined, then spoon the batter into the prepared muffin tin.

4   Bake for about 20 minutes until risen and golden. Leave to cool in the tin for a few minutes, then transfer to a wire rack to cool.

5   To decorate, put the candy cane or rock in a plastic bag and tap with a rolling pin to break into pieces. Set aside. Stir together the icing sugar and lemon juice until smooth, then add a few drops of food colouring to tint the icing, if you like. Spoon on top of the muffins and sprinkle pieces of candy cane or rock on top.

Carrot Cupcakes with Honey Orange Frosting

This is a lovely carrot cake recipe simply baked as little cupcakes. If you have your own special recipe, do try it as cupcakes rather than one cake. Carrot cake is usually iced with a honey and cream cheese topping, and these cakes are no exception. Look for a good-quality cream cheese; a light or soft version will not work as well.

175g (6oz) soft brown sugar
175ml (6fl oz) sunflower oil
3 large free-range eggs
140g (5oz) plain flour
1½ teaspoons bicarbonate of soda
1½ teaspoons baking powder
1 teaspoon ground cinnamon
½ teaspoon freshly grated nutmeg
A pinch of salt
225g (8oz) grated or shredded carrot

For the cream cheese icing
225g (8oz) curd/cream cheese
   (not soft or light cream cheese),
   softened
2 teaspoons clear honey
   (or more to taste)
Grated zest of 1 unwaxed orange
Orange sprinkles to decorate

1 Preheat the oven to 180°C, 350°F, gas mark 4. Grease and line a muffin tin with paper cases.

2 Mix the sugar and oil in a large bowl. Add the eggs and mix well. Sift in the dry ingredients and beat everything together until really well combined. Next add the grated carrots and stir through well.

3 Place spoonfuls of batter into the prepared cases and bake in the oven for 15–20 minutes. If the tops are getting too browned and it looks like the insides are still raw, cover with baking paper and cook for a little longer. Remove from the oven and leave to cool.

4 While they are cooling, make the icing. Put the cream cheese in a bowl, and beat until softened. Stir in the honey and orange zest. Taste to make sure it is sweet enough and add a little more honey if you want. When the cakes are cold, spread the icing over the top and decorate with sprinkles.

Battenburg Cupcakes

The Battenburg is another popular bake that works beautifully as individual cakes, and you can play around with the colour combinations to suit your crockery! The tang of the apricot jam makes for a good contrast with the icing but you could use any other flavour.

225g (8oz) self-raising flour
225g (8oz) caster sugar
225g (8oz) margarine, softened
2 teaspoons baking powder
4 large free-range eggs
2 teaspoons pure vanilla extract
Pink food colouring (preferably gel)
Apricot jam for spreading
1 quantity lemon glacé icing
   (see page 16)
Dolly mixture or other sprinkles to
   decorate

1   Preheat the oven to 160°C, 325°F, gas mark 3. Grease and line two 20cm (8in) square cake tins.

2   Sift the flour and sugar into a mixing bowl. Add the margarine, baking powder, eggs and vanilla and beat until light and fluffy. Divide the batter into two equal portions in separate bowls, and add a few drops of pink food colouring to one half. Pour each cake batter into a separate tin, and bake in the oven for 20–25 minutes until firm to the touch and golden. Don't worry that the pink cake doesn't look very pink.

3   Remove from the oven and turn both cakes out onto wire racks to cool. Using a sharp knife, level the tops of the cakes so that the top and the bottom are completely flat. Spread a thin layer of apricot jam over the upper side of the pink layer. Place the plain cake on top so that the bottom side of the sponge faces upwards. Cut into 1.5cm (¾in) strips.

4   Now, lay one strip on its side so that you have a line of pink and a line of yellow. Spread a thin layer of jam over the top. Take another strip of cake and lay it on its side on top of the jam strip, but reversed so that yellow lies directly on top of pink and vice versa. Cut these strips into squares, and drizzle with the glacé icing. Let some of the icing dribble down the sides. Pop a dolly mixture (or alternative adornment) on top, and place in paper cases.

Mini Cherry Tarts

A version of the delicious cherry Bakewell tart, this miniature variation must feature in many people's top ten small cakes. This recipe also has the benefit of having no fat and no flour, but is packed with healthy fruit and nuts. As a result, they make a perfectly wonderful for treat for anyone who is gluten-intolerant.

4 large free-range eggs, separated
175g (6oz) caster sugar
225g (8oz) ground almonds
1 teaspoon baking powder (or
   ½ teaspoon bicarbonate of soda
   and 1 teaspoon cream of tartar if
   you want to keep it gluten-free)
12 glacé cherries

For the decoration
1 quantity lemon glacé icing
   (see page 212)
Golf-ball-sized piece of
   rolled fondant
Red food colouring (preferably gel)
Edible glue
Red edible glitter
Green food colouring (preferably gel)
1 tablespoon royal icing
   (see page 213)
Icing bag

1 Preheat the oven to 200°F, 400°F, gas mark 6. Line a 12-hole muffin tin with paper cases.

2 Beat the egg yolks and sugar together in a large bowl until light and fluffy. In a clean, dry separate bowl, whisk the egg whites until stiff peaks form. Gently fold them into the egg yolk mixture, then fold in the ground almonds and baking powder. Spoon the batter into the prepared cases, and push 1 cherry down into each sponge. Bake in the oven for 15–20 minutes until risen and golden. Keep an eye on them so that they don't over-cook. Remove from the oven and leave to cool.

3 Pour a little glacé icing over each cake. While you are waiting for the icing to set (30 minutes), make the rolled fondant cherries. Dye the fondant red by dipping a cocktail stick into the red food colouring and transferring it to the fondant. Knead the colour in evenly, then make little cherry-sized balls (one for each cupcake), paint them with the edible glue and roll them in the edible glitter.

4 When the icing is dry, add a little food colouring to the royal icing to make it green. Fill an icing bag with the royal icing, squeezing down to the end. Snip the very end off the bag. Stick a fondant cherry onto each cupcake with a tiny blob of edible glue, and pipe stalks and leaves with the green royal icing.

Ultimate Cupcakes

Who needs an excuse to bake something scrumptious?
Whether it's Valentine's Day, Mother's Day or a children's party,
cupcakes can be dressed up for any special occasion.

Cupcake base
12 cupcakes

100g (4oz) self-raising flour
100g (4oz) caster sugar
100g (4oz) margarine, softened
1 teaspoon baking powder
2 large free-range eggs
1 teaspoon pure vanilla extract

1 Preheat the oven to 160°C, 325°F, gas mark 3. Line a 12-hole muffin tin with paper cases.

2 Put all the ingredients in a large bowl or mixer bowl and mix thoroughly until the batter is light and fluffy. Put heaped teaspoons of the batter into the prepared cases, and bake in the oven for about 20 minutes until golden, and firm and springy when you give them a light press on top.

3 Remove from the oven and transfer to a wire rack to cool before preparing the icing.

English summer cupcakes
12 cupcakes

This recipe works well as a dessert after a lovely summery lunch. This is one of those recipes that can look very elegant, but is easy to make.

1 quantity cupcake base
   (see left)
250g (9oz) mascarpone cheese
Selection of soft ripe fruit such
   as blueberries, strawberries,
   raspberries, peaches and nectarines

1 Make the cupcakes from the recipe on the left, then leave them to cool.

2 Empty the tub of mascarpone cheese into a bowl and beat lightly to soften. Place a spoonful of mascarpone on top of each of the cupcakes, and artfully arrange the fruit on and around the cakes.

Use the cupcake base recipe and follow these simple instructions for different looks!

Mother's Day delights
12 cupcakes

You can buy pre-made sugar roses in cake decorating shops and online if you are pushed for time. Whatever you decide, these cupcakes will make a spectacular treat for Mother's Day.

200g (7oz) icing sugar, sifted
Boiling water
Gel food colouring
12 sugared roses

1 Make the cupcakes from the recipe on the left and leave to cool. To make the icing, put the icing sugar in a bowl, and gradually add boiling water until you have a thick soup consistency. Stir constantly. Add the food colouring, then pour over the cakes. Wait about 10 minutes before carefully placing a rose on top of each cupcake.

Fashion cupcakes
12 cupcakes

These fun little cakes are guaranteed to get the party started.

Pink and dark brown gel food colouring
1 quantity of glacé icing
   (see page 16)
2 tablespoons royal icing
   (see page 17)

1 Make the cupcakes from the recipe on the left and leave to cool. Tint the glacé icing pink and use to ice the cooled cupcakes. Leave to dry for at least 1 hour. Tint half the royal icing dark brown. If it gets too runny, add some more sifted icing sugar. Put the brown royal icing in a icing bag with a fine nozzle and the remaining white royal icing into another one.

2 With the brown royal icing, pipe 1950-style dresses (small waists, large skirts) onto a few cakes, high heeled shoes on a few more and handbags onto yet more. If you are stuck for ideas, look in a few magazines or draw out some examples first. Fill in patterns and folds on the dresses, buckles and pockets on the bags, and stitch lines and other details on the shoes with the white royal icing.

Simple heart cupcakes
12 cupcakes

Yes, there is some piping here. No, it isn't tricky. Royal icing is invaluable for piping. You can use it for icing cakes if you like a very hard surface. If you are a bit nervous about your piping skills, practise on a plate or directly onto your work surface. When you are happy that you have the flow of the shape right, make a start. Let the base layer of icing dry before you start decorating. If you want to create something other than hearts, do it. Tiny spots all over look really pretty and couldn't be simpler.

1 quantity cupcake base
  (see page 122)
1 quantity glacé icing
  (see page 16)
2 tablespoons royal icing
  (see page 17)
Food colourings (preferably gel)
Icing bag

1 Make the cupcakes from the recipe on page 122 and leave them to cool.

2 Spoon the icing over the cakes and leave to set. Leaving them for a 1-2 hours at this stage is best, if you can.

3 Tint the royal icing with the food colouring, then use some to fill the icing bag, squeezing it down to the end.

4 Snip the very end off the bag. Practise piping the hearts or whatever shape you want, then pipe your chosen shape on the top of each iced cupcake. Leave to dry for another hour or so before eating.

Gadzooks for the spooks
12 cupcakes

Black Hallowe'en cupcakes are highly entertaining. Black icing is wonderful – it transforms your teeth and mouth at first bite. There is absolutely no room for subtlety here. You can scare trick-or-treaters by having a mouthful of cake just before you open the door. Rest assured that the colour does fade quite rapidly …

1 quantity cupcake base
(see page 122)
1 quantity glacé icing
(see page 16)
Black and orange food colouring
(preferably gel)
Golf ball-sized piece of rolled fondant
Edible glue

1 Make the cupcakes from the recipe on page 122 and allow to cool. Make up the glacé icing, and divide into two portions; use the food colouring to make one black and the other deep orange. Divide the cupcakes into two batches, and ice one batch black and the other batch orange. Leave them to dry. (These cakes need to be completely dry before you add anything else because of the dark colours.)

2 Take a third of the rolled fondant and tint it black. Make a ghost by flattening out a piece of white fondant into the shape of a ghost and use edible glue to stick it onto a black-iced cupcake. Let the ghost trail over the edge of the cake in a ghostly manner. Take some tiny bits of black paste, and stick them on to make a ghoulish face for the ghost.

3 Make the spider by taking a bit of black paste the size of a broad bean and sticking it onto an orange-iced cake using edible glue. Make as many legs as you can (8 is traditional!) out of slivers of black paste, and stick them on. You can also add a final strip of black for the web. A face and fangs made out of white rolled fondant finishes it off.

4 For the spooky eyes, take 2 elongated egg shapes of white rolled fondant, add black pupils and stick onto a black-iced cake.

Hallowe'en super scaries

18–20 cupcakes

Hallowe'en is the time of year to roast some squash or pumpkin and then throw it into these irresistibly sweet and spicy little cakes. Look out for fake spiders and other nasties in kids' toy shops and hide a few on the plate to scare anyone else away ... leaving you with a large batch of cupcakes all to yourself!

200g (7oz) peeled, seeded pumpkin,
  cut into chunks
½ tablespoon sunflower oil
300g (10oz) plain flour
1 tablespoon baking powder
1 teaspoon ground cinnamon
1 large free-range egg, beaten
50ml (2fl oz) soured cream
3–4 tablespoons milk
100g (4oz) soft brown sugar
60g (2½oz) butter, melted

To decorate
150g (5oz) white chocolate
25g (1oz) plain chocolate

1 Preheat the oven to 190°C, 375°F, gas mark 5.

2 Put the pumpkin in a baking dish, drizzle with the oil, then toss to coat. Roast for about 35 minutes until tender. Remove from the oven and leave to cool, then mash roughly with a fork.

3 To make the cupcakes, preheat the oven to 200°C, 400°F, gas mark 6. Line two 12-hole muffin tins with paper cases. Combine the flour, baking powder and cinnamon and sift into a large bowl. In a separate bowl, combine the egg, soured cream, milk, mashed pumpkin, sugar and butter and stir together until well mixed. Pour into the dry ingredients and stir together until just combined, then spoon large dollops of the batter into the prepared muffin tin.

4 Bake for about 15 minutes until risen and golden. Leave to cool in the tin for a few minutes, then turn out onto a wire rack.

5 To decorate, melt the white chocolate in a heatproof bowl set over a pan of barely simmering water, then spoon on top of the cakes. Melt the plain chocolate in the same way in a separate bowl, then spoon into a icing bag with a very narrow tube. Pipe concentric circles onto each cake, then use a skewer to draw a line from the centre to the outside of each cake to make a spider's web pattern.

Easter muffins
12 muffins

When you're celebrating Easter with a gluten- or dairy-intolerant cake-eater, this is the recipe to choose. Inspired by the fruity marzipan simnel cake, these little muffins look cuter than cute topped off with baby chick yellow icing and pastel-coloured eggs. Be sure to check the ingredients on your pastel-coloured eggs and marzipan to make sure they don't contain any dairy or gluten.

200g (7oz) potato flour
100g (4oz) rice flour
1 tablespoon cornflour
1 tablespoon gluten-free baking
  powder
100g (4oz) caster sugar
100g (4oz) raisins or sultanas
2 tablespoons candied peel
1 large free-range egg, beaten
175ml (6fl oz) soya milk
6 tablespoons sunflower oil
100g (4oz) gluten-free marzipan,
  finely grated
Finely grated zest of 1 lemon

To decorate
200g (7oz) icing sugar, sifted
2 tablespoons lemon juice
Yellow food colouring
Pastel-coloured mini eggs

1 Preheat the oven to 200°C, 400°F, gas mark 6. Grease or line a 12-hole muffin tin.

2 Combine the flours, baking powder and caster sugar and sift into a large bowl, then add the raisins or sultanas and candied peel.

3 In a separate bowl or jug, combine the egg, milk and oil, then stir in the marzipan and lemon zest. Pour into the dry ingredients and stir together until just combined, then spoon large dollops of the batter into the prepared muffin tin.

4 Bake for about 20 minutes until risen and golden. Leave to cool in the tin for a few minutes, then turn out onto a wire rack to cool.

5 To decorate, mix the icing sugar and lemon juice until smooth, then add a few drops of food colouring to make a pale yellow icing. Spoon on top of the cakes and top with mini eggs.

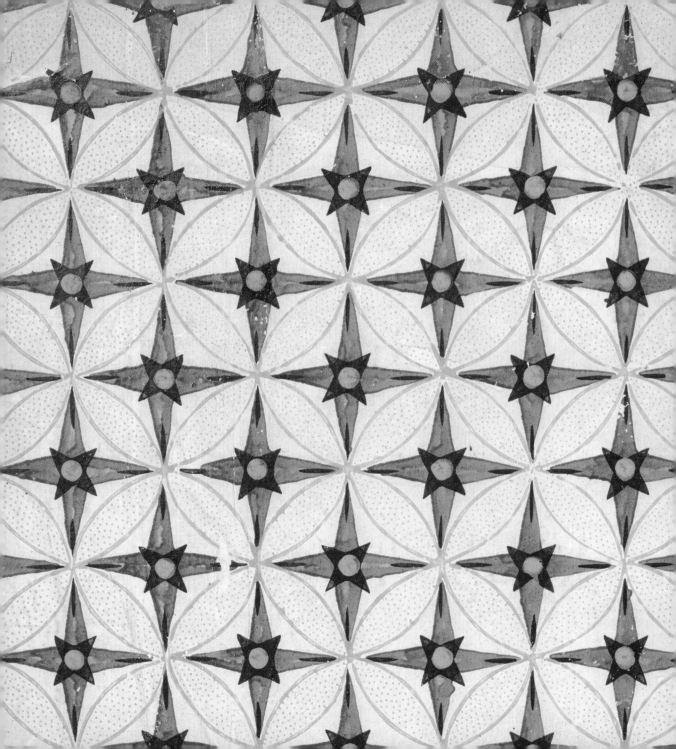

Fun for
Little Ones

Jam Doughnuts

For those who love doughnuts but don't own a deep-fat fryer and are wary of having a heavy pan of boiling fat on the hob, this recipe is the solution. You simply bake them. These really taste like doughnuts and are (slightly!) better for you because they are baked rather than deep-fried.

200g (7oz) strong white bread flour
¼ teaspoon salt
200g (7oz) caster sugar
25g (1oz) butter
7g (¼oz) fast-action dried yeast
  (to substitute fresh yeast, see
  page 216)
5 tablespoons milk
1 large free-range egg, beaten
4 tablespoons strawberry jam (or jam
  of your choice)
50g (2oz) icing sugar

1 Lightly grease a baking sheet.

2 Put the bread flour, the salt and 4 tablespoons of the caster sugar into a large bowl and rub in the butter until it looks like fine breadcrumbs, then stir in the yeast. Heat the milk until it is warm – so that when you dip in your finger it feels neither warm nor cold. Mix the milk and the egg into the flour mixture until it forms a dough.

3 Turn the dough on to a lightly floured work surface and knead the dough until it is elastic and no longer sticky, adding a little extra flour to your hands or the work surface as necessary.

4 Put the dough back in the bowl and cover it with a tea towel. Leave in a warm place for about 1 hour, or until doubled in size.

5 Take the dough out and give it another knead for a couple of minutes, then cut it into 12 equal pieces. Roll each ball out to a circle of about 10cm (4in) in diameter and put a smallish teaspoon of jam right in the centre. Gather up the edges of the circle around the jam and pinch it all together to make a seal. Place the filled doughnut seal-side down on a baking sheet and repeat the process, leaving lots of space between each one. Cover again with the tea towel and leave to rise for 45 minutes.

6 Preheat the oven to 180°C, 350°F, gas mark 4. Bake the doughnuts for 10 minutes, or until beautifully golden. Remove from the oven and leave to cool for a minute or so while you make the glaze.

7 Mix the icing sugar with enough water to make a thin, runny icing and brush it over each doughnut. Put the remaining caster sugar in a deep dish and roll the doughnuts in it until covered. Serve immediately.

Rock Buns

The key element to any decent fête, school cake sale or homemade cake competition, rock buns are an all-time favourite with a cup of tea. Rock-like in appearance but not in texture, this unsophisticated little favourite is easy to make and always welcome on the tea table. You can make them as large or as small as you like, so you may make fewer, or more, than the 12 indicated.

225g (8oz) plain wholemeal flour
100g (4oz) plain flour
4 teaspoons baking powder
1 teaspoon mixed spice
1 teaspoon freshly grated nutmeg
175g (6oz) unsalted butter, softened
75g (3oz) light soft brown sugar
175g (6oz) mixed dried fruit
1 large free-range egg, beaten
1–2 tablespoons milk
Caster sugar for dusting

1 Preheat the oven to 220°C, 425°F, gas mark 7 and grease and line two baking sheets.

2 Mix together the flours, baking powder and spices in a bowl, then rub in the butter until the mixture resembles breadcrumbs.

3 Add the sugar and fruit and mix well. Add the egg and 1 tablespoon of the milk, and mix until you have a stiff but moist dough. Add the remaining milk if you need to.

4 Using two forks, drop the batter in 12 heaps on the baking sheets. Sprinkle a little caster sugar over the top and bake for about 20 minutes, or until they are golden brown.

5 Remove from the oven and transfer to a wire rack to cool.

Play around with the sizes of these and see which you like best!

Fondant Fancies

20 fancies

These delicate little iced cakes are a popular choice for tea time or parties, especially as you can make them in different colours. They look beautiful decorated with summer flowers.

175g (6oz) soft margarine
175g (6oz) self-raising flour
175g (6oz) caster sugar
3 large free-range eggs
1½ teaspoons pure vanilla extract
75g (3oz) unsalted butter, softened
350g (12oz) icing sugar, sifted
Food colouring

1 Preheat the oven to 160°C, 325°F, gas mark 3. Grease and line a 20cm (8in) square cake tin.

2 Put the margarine, flour, caster sugar, eggs and 1 tablespoon vanilla extract into a large bowl and beat until the batter is light and fluffy. Pour it into the prepared tin and bake for about 20 minutes, or until firm and springy to the touch and a skewer inserted in the centre comes out clean. Remove from the oven and turn out onto a wire rack to cool.

3 Meanwhile, make the buttercream. Cream together the butter and 150g (5oz) of the icing sugar with the remaining vanilla until pale and creamy. You may need to add a drop of milk if the mixture is really stiff – you need a piping consistency. Put the buttercream into an icing bag fitted with a plain tube.

4 Cut the cold cake into squares and pipe a small blob of buttercream into the centre of each cake. Let the buttercream dry for a minute or two while you make the icing.

5 Mix a small amount of water into the remaining icing sugar until you have an icing that thickly coats the back of a spoon. If it is too runny, add more icing sugar; too thick, add a drop more water. Tint the icing whatever colour you like. Put the cakes on a wire rack over a tray and spoon the icing over the top of each cake so that it runs down the sides. You may need to tease it over the corners, but let the icing do the work for you. Leave the cakes to dry on the rack for an hour.

6 Make up a little more icing if you wish and drizzle a contrasting zigzag line across each cake. You can do this directly from a spoon or with an icing bag. Lay out the required number of round paper cases and open them out slightly. Place each cake in a case and wrap the edges of the cases round the cakes. If you do this while the icing is slightly tacky, it will stick.

Cherry Buns

This was traditionally a favourite recipe to encourage kids to make a lot of mess with a large bowl and a wooden spoon. Modern children love making them as much as ever and become equally absorbed in the baking process. The icing is a grown-up addition.

75g (3oz) margarine
75g (3oz) caster sugar
1 large free-range egg
125g (4½oz) self-raising flour
Grated zest of 1 unwaxed lemon
150g (5oz) glacé cherries
2–3 tablespoons milk
200g (7oz) icing sugar, sifted
4 tablespoons boiling water

1 Preheat the oven to 180°C, 350°F, gas mark 4. Line a 12-hole muffin tin with paper cases.

2 Cream the margarine and sugar until the mixture is light and creamy, using a wooden spoon or a mixer. Beat in the egg.

3 Sift the flour into a second bowl and add the lemon zest. Reserve 12 of the cherries. Quarter the remainder, add to the flour and mix in. Add the flour to the creamed mixture and stir well so that all the ingredients are thoroughly blended.

4 Add enough milk to make the batter just soft enough to drop from the spoon. Spoon into the prepared cases and bake for 20–25 minutes.

5 Remove from the oven and turn out onto a wire rack to cool.

6 Put the icing sugar in a bowl and gradually add the water a little at a time, stirring vigorously until you have a thick icing. Spoon over the cakes and top with a cherry to finish.

These jaunty little buns look great in patterned cases!

Gingerbread Playground

12 biscuits

This dough is easy to make and bakes to a lovely biscuit that is crunchy but not too hard. You can use it for an ordinary biscuit, of course, but the gingerbread people are more fun! Once they are baked, you can really go to town with the decorations. Forget the traditional eyes, nose and three buttons and let the kids introduce some colour and imagination.

350g (12oz) plain flour (but you may need more)
1 teaspoon bicarbonate of soda
2 teaspoons ground ginger
100g (4oz) butter
175g (6oz) soft light brown sugar
1 large free-range egg
4 tablespoons golden syrup
4 tablespoons royal icing (see page 17)
Food colouring gels
Silver dragées
Several icing bags and size 2 tubes

1 Sift the flour, bicarbonate of soda and ginger into a large bowl. Add the butter and rub it in with your fingertips until you have a mixture resembling fine breadcrumbs. Add the sugar and mix well.

2 In another bowl, beat the egg and golden syrup together using a balloon whisk. Tip the mixture over the flour and stir well. You may find it easier to use your hands at this point. Sometimes the dough can be a bit on the sticky side. Keep sprinkling over flour and working it in until you have a lovely smooth dough.

3 Wrap the dough in cling film and leave to chill in the fridge for at least 30 minutes, but an hour would be better.

4 Preheat the oven to 190°C, 375°F, gas mark 5 and line two baking sheets with baking parchment.

5 Roll out the dough on a lightly floured surface to a thickness of about 5mm (¼in). Cut out the required shapes, place them slightly apart on your lined baking sheets and bake for 12–15 minutes until golden.

6 Remove from the oven and leave to cool on the baking sheets for 5 minutes before transferring them to a wire rack to cool completely.

7 To decorate, divide the royal icing into as many colours as you want and tint with the gels. Place each coloured royal icing in a separate icing bag and decorate to your heart's content. Create 2 dots for eyes and place the silver dragées on top. Let the biscuits dry before serving.

Lemon Biscuits

Lemon and almond go particularly well together. These are really easy to make and, as an added extra, they don't even need rolling out. They are also very versatile. Don't eat them while warm: the lemon curd will still be molten hot!

100g (4oz) caster sugar
200g (7oz) butter, softened
60g (2¼oz) icing sugar, sifted
1 large free-range egg yolk
150g (5oz) ground almonds
1 teaspoon almond extract
Finely grated zest and juice of
   1 large unwaxed lemon
300g (10oz) plain flour
1 teaspoon baking powder
150g (5oz) jar of lemon curd

1 Preheat the oven to 190°C, 375°F, gas mark 5 and line two baking sheets with baking parchment.

2 Beat the caster sugar and butter together in a large bowl until very light and fluffy. Beat in the icing sugar, egg yolk, ground almonds, almond extract, lemon zest and 2 teaspoons of the lemon juice. Beat it all together well. Sift in the flour and baking powder and stir until everything is combined.

3 Shape pieces of the mixture into balls just a bit smaller than a golf ball and place on the prepared baking sheets, spaced well apart. With your thumb, press down to form a little well in the now flattened ball and fill with a little dollop of lemon curd (not too much or it will overflow and burn).

4 Bake for about 10–12 minutes until the biscuits are golden and gorgeous.

5 Remove from the oven and transfer to a wire rack to cool completely before serving.

Ginger Biscuits

12 biscuits

These are unsophisticated, gorgeously moreish biscuits with a fabulous aroma of ground ginger and are very popular with both children and adults. They are the perfect biscuit for the little ones to make.

150g (5oz) self-raising flour
½ teaspoon bicarbonate of soda
2 teaspoons ground ginger
1 teaspoon ground cinnamon
2 teaspoons caster sugar
50g (2oz) butter
2 tablespoons golden syrup

1 Preheat the oven to 190°C, 375°F, gas mark 5 and line two baking sheets with baking parchment.

2 Sift together all the dry ingredients in a large bowl. Heat the butter and golden syrup gently in a pan and when the butter has melted, pour it over the dry ingredients. Mix well until you have a soft dough. If it's a little bit sticky, sprinkle a little more flour onto it until you get a consistency you can comfortably handle.

3 Using your hands, form small balls of the mixture, flatten them slightly and place them on the prepared baking sheets, spaced well apart. Bake for about 15 minutes until golden.

4 Remove from the oven and leave to cool for 5 minutes on the baking sheets before transferring them onto a wire rack to cool completely.

These biscuits make great gifts: simply wrap in clean baking parchment and tie with a ribbon.

Chocolate Chip Shortbread

12 biscuits

This is a really easy way of jazzing up plain shortbread. If you're feeling adventurous you could experiment with different flavoured chocolate chips.

250g (9oz) butter, softened
50g (2oz) caster sugar
250g (9oz) plain flour
125g (4½oz) cornflour
50g (2oz) chunky chocolate chips

1 Cream together the butter and sugar in a large bowl until light and fluffy. Sift the flour and cornflour onto the butter mixture and mix until you have a lovely smooth dough.

2 Sprinkle the chocolate chips over the dough and knead in with your hands until the chocolate is evenly distributed.

3 Roll out a sheet of cling film, tip the dough onto it, then form the dough into a fat sausage and wrap up tightly. Leave to chill in the refrigerator for at least an hour.

4 Preheat the oven to 160°C, 325°F, gas mark 3 and line two baking sheets with baking parchment.

5 Remove the roll of dough from its cling film and slice into circles. Place the circles on the prepared baking sheets and bake for about 30 minutes until they are pale golden.

6 Remove from the oven and leave to cool for 5 minutes on the baking sheets before transferring onto a wire rack to cool completely.

Rocky Roadsters

Although the rocky road combination of nuts, marshmallows and chocolate usually goes into ice cream, there's no reason why you shouldn't throw the trio into a muffin instead. If you do, you'll find yourself with an irresistible batch of the squishiest, meltiest, chunkiest muffins you've ever seen.

300g (10oz) self-raising flour
1 teaspoon baking powder
3 tablespoons cocoa powder
75g (3oz) milk chocolate, chopped
75g (3oz) walnut pieces
50g (2oz) mini marshmallows
   (or large marshmallows snipped
   into pieces)
150g (5oz) soft brown sugar
200ml (7fl oz) milk
2 large free-range eggs, beaten
75g (3oz) butter, melted

1   Preheat the oven to 200°C, 400°F, gas mark 6. Grease a 12-hole muffin tin or line with paper cases.

2   Combine the flour, baking powder and cocoa and sift into a large bowl. Reserve about one-third of the chocolate chunks and nuts, then add the rest, along with the marshmallows, to the flour.

3   In a separate bowl or jug, combine the sugar, milk, eggs and butter, then pour into the dry ingredients. Stir together until just combined, then divide the mixture evenly into the prepared muffin tin. Gently press the reserved chocolate and nuts at random into the muffins.

4   Bake for about 20 minutes until risen and firm to the touch. Remove from the oven and leave to cool in the tin for a few minutes, then turn out onto a wire rack to cool completely.

Chirpy Chirpy Cheep Cheep

12 cakes

Those lovely little fluffy yellow chicks appear in shops just before Easter, so if you don't want to do anything other than ice some cupcakes, you could stand one of these chicks on top. Just make sure that no one thinks that they are edible. Otherwise these simple piped chicks look lovely. Pastel colours make the best backgrounds.

100g (4oz) self-raising flour
100g (4oz) caster sugar
100g (4oz) margarine, softened
1 teaspoon baking powder
2 large free-range eggs
1 teaspoon pure vanilla extract

For the decoration
1 quantity of glacé icing (see page 16) tinted in pastel colours with gel food colouring
2 tablespoons royal icing (see page 17) plus 1 tablespoon green royal icing (optional) yellow, black and orange gel food colouring
3 icing bags with fine tubes

1 Preheat the oven to 160°C, 325°F, gas mark 3. Line a 12-hole muffin tin with paper cases.

2 Put all the ingredients (except the decoration) in a food processor. Mix well until the batter is light and fluffy. Put heaped teaspoons of the batter into the prepared cases, and bake in the oven for about 20 minutes until golden, and firm and springy when lightly pressed.

3 Remove from the oven and turn out onto a wire rack to cool.

4 Ice the cooled cupcakes with a selection of pastel-coloured icings in glacé. Leave them to dry.

5 Split the royal icing into thirds. Take two-thirds and tint it yellow. Fill an icing bag with the yellow royal icing, and push to the end. To make a fluffy chick, pipe a chick shape onto the cake, and fill in the chick with random squiggles of yellow royal icing. Make sure that you go ever so slightly over your outline, so that the chick looks fluffy. To make a flatter chick, again pipe an outline. Thin out some of the yellow royal icing with a few drops of water so that you have a consistency a little thicker than double cream. Carefully fill in the outline with this mixture, and leave to dry completely.

6 When both are dry, divide the remaining royal icing into two, and tint one portion black and the other orange. Fill two separate decorating bags, one with each colour. Pipe an eye on each chick with the black royal icing, and a beak with the orange.

7 With the green royal icing, pipe tiny spots all the way round the outer edge of the cupcakes.

Party Time!

Kids' parties are great fun for the little ones – but not without some stress for the parents! With these fantastic recipes and decorating ideas you'll be sure to have the delicious party treats covered – now all you need is some party games.

Lemony lustres
12 cupcakes

Edible lustre comes as a powder from sugarcraft shops. Be sure to check that it is edible and not just safe to use for removable cake decorations!

100g (4oz) butter, softened
100g (4oz) caster sugar
2 large free-range eggs, beaten
100g (4oz) self-raising flour
1 teaspoon baking powder
Grated zest of 1 unwaxed lemon
1 tablespoon freshly squeezed lemon juice

For the decoration
1 quantity glacé icing (page 16)
Gel food colouring (optional)
1 tablespoon royal icing (see page 17)
Edible lustre (available from cake decorating and sugarcraft stores)
½ teaspoon vodka or other clear alcohol

1 Preheat the oven to 160°C, 325°F, gas mark 3. Line a 12-hole muffin tin with paper cases.

2 Cream the butter and sugar together until light and fluffy. Gradually add the beaten eggs, beating well after each addition. Sift the flour and baking powder onto the mixture and, using a large metal spoon, carefully fold it in. Add the lemon zest and, if the batter looks a little stiff, fold in the juice a little at a time (it may not be needed) until you have a soft batter.

3 Spoon into the prepared cases and bake for 20–25 minutes until golden and firm to the touch. Remove from the oven and turn out onto a wire rack to cool.

4 Tint the glacé icing and spoon over the cooled cakes. When the icing has dried, put the royal icing into a icing bag with a fine tube, and pipe a large heart onto each cupcake. Wait for this to harden slightly, which will take about an hour.

5 To finish, tip ½ teaspoon of the lustre onto a saucer or into a small bowl. Add some vodka to the lustre drop by drop. Mix with the paintbrush until you have a consistency just a tiny bit looser than a paste. Leave the alcohol to evaporate – the mixture will thicken up slightly. Carefully brush the lustre mixture over the piped heart and let it dry.

For a fun kids' party, provide the guests with icing and sprinkles to transform plain cupcakes into their very own masterpieces!

Superhero cakes
12 cupcakes

These colourful offerings will always be on hand to save the day!

1 quantity cupcake base recipe (see page 122)
1 quantity glacé icing (see page 16)
Gel food colouring in assorted colours
2 tablespoons royal icing (see page 17)
3 icing bags fitted with fine tubes

1 Make the cupcakes from the recipe on page 122 and leave to cool.

2 Make the glacé icing with the icing sugar and either lemon juice or water. Colour the icing deep blue or green or brown. Cover the cakes with the icing and let them dry really well. With colour this dark, it is important that the icing is as dry as possible before you start decorating otherwise the colours will bleed into each other.

3 Divide the royal icing into three bowls, and tint them whatever colour you prefer. The royal icing needs to be really firm, so if it's a bit runny add a little more sifted icing sugar. Pipe on comic-strip words, such as 'BIFF', 'POW' and 'ZAP'.

Butterflies go disco
12 cupcakes

You can buy interestingly shaped cutters to use for biscuits or also for rolled-out icing. You can see some imaginative ideas for decorations in the picture.

1 quantity cupcake base recipe
  (see page 122)
1 quantity glacé icing (see page 16)
Gel food colouring in assorted colours
Cornflour for dusting
Golf ball-sized piece of rolled fondant
Edible glue
Edible glitter

1 Make the cupcakes from the recipe on page 122 and leave to cool. Colour the glacé icing as you wish. Pour over the cakes and leave to dry.

2 Dust a little cornflour onto a work surface, and roll out the rolled fondant until it is about 3mm (⅛in) thick. Cut out butterflies using cutters – allow one large or two small butterflies per cake.

3 Brush a little edible glue all over the butterflies. Pour the edible glitter onto a plate and dip the butterflies in the glitter to coat.

4 Stick the butterflies to the cakes. If you are using two small ones, it looks lovely if you have them flying off in different directions.

Peanut butter & choc chip cheekies

12 cupcakes

Children just love these large, fat muffins studded with chocolate chips and little nuggets of peanut. If you want to go for a dairy-free version, use bittersweet chocolate chips and substitute soya milk for cow's milk.

300g (10oz) self-raising flour
1 teaspoon baking powder
100g (4oz) milk chocolate chips
200g (7oz) crunchy peanut butter
100g (4oz) soft brown sugar
2 large free-range eggs, beaten
200ml (7fl oz) milk

1 Preheat the oven to 200°C, 400°F, gas mark 6. Grease a 12-hole muffin tin or line with paper cases.

2 Combine the flour and baking powder and sift into a large bowl, then add about three-quarters of the chocolate chips.

3 In a separate bowl, beat together the peanut butter and sugar, then gradually beat in the eggs and milk to make a smooth mixture. Pour into the dry ingredients and stir together until just combined, then spoon large dollops into the prepared muffin tin. Sprinkle with the remaining chocolate chips, pressing them gently into the batter. Bake for about 18 minutes until risen and golden.

4 Remove from the oven and leave to cool in the tin for a few minutes, before turning out onto a wire rack to cool completely.

Beetroot bonanza

12 cupcakes

Don't be put off if you don't like beetroot, these perfectly pink muffins are not a million miles away from a carrot-cakey muffin – sweet, tender, moreish and, even better, bright pink! Serve them with a simple swirl of icing or, for something a bit more special, look out for pink sugar sprinkles to scatter over the top.

300g (10oz) plain flour
1 tablespoon baking powder
150g (5oz) caster sugar
1 teaspoon ground cinnamon
½ teaspoon ground ginger
200ml (7fl oz) milk
2 large free-range eggs, beaten
100ml (4fl oz) vegetable oil
1 large beetroot, grated, about
*   100g (4oz)*

For the icing

150g (5oz) cream cheese
4½ tablespoons icing sugar
1 teaspoon lemon juice
Pink food colouring gel
Sprinkles to decorate (optional)

1 Preheat the oven to 200°C, 400°F, gas mark 6. Grease a 12-hole muffin tin or line with paper cases.

2 Combine the flour, baking powder, caster sugar, cinnamon and ginger and sift into a large bowl.

3 In a separate bowl, combine the milk, eggs and oil, then stir in the beetroot so that the mixture turns bright pink. Pour into the dry ingredients and stir together until just combined, then spoon large dollops of the batter into the prepared muffin tin.

4 Bake for about 20 minutes until risen and firm to the touch.

5 Remove from the oven and leave to cool in the tin for a few minutes, before turning out onto a wire rack to cool completely.

6 To serve, beat together the cream cheese, icing sugar and lemon juice until smooth and creamy. Add a few drops of pink food colouring to make a vibrant pink icing, then swirl on top of the muffins. Decorate with sprinkles, if you like.

Coloured sweeties

12 muffins

These muffins will appeal to little ones as much as older children – particularly the way the sweets turn the muffins rainbow-coloured once they've been baked. Younger children can help with spooning on the icing and sticking on the sweets, while older children can help with the baking.

300g (10oz) self-raising flour
1 teaspoon baking powder
100g (4oz) caster sugar
50g (2oz) M&Ms or Smarties
200ml (7fl oz) buttermilk
1 large free-range egg, beaten
1 teaspoon pure vanilla extract
75g (3oz) butter, melted

To decorate
5 tablespoons soured cream
100g (4oz) icing sugar, sifted
50g (2oz) M&Ms or Smarties

1 Preheat the oven to 190°C, 375°F, gas mark 5. Grease a 12-hole muffin tin or line with paper cases.

2 Combine the flour, baking powder and caster sugar and sift into a large bowl, then add the M&Ms.

3 In a separate bowl or jug, lightly beat the buttermilk, egg and vanilla to combine, then stir in the butter. Pour into the dry ingredients and stir together until just combined, then spoon large dollops of the batter into the prepared muffin tin.

4 Bake for about 20 minutes until risen and golden.

5 Remove from the oven and leave to cool in the tin for a few minutes, before turning out onto a wire rack to cool completely.

6 To decorate, beat the soured cream and icing sugar together until creamy, then spoon over the muffins. Decorate with more M&Ms on top.

Birthday mini muffins

24 muffins

Who needs a big birthday cake when there are mini, bitesize muffins to gobble instead? With twenty-four muffins in each batch, they're perfect for a party.

300g (10oz) self-raising flour
1 teaspoon baking powder
2 tablespoons cocoa powder, plus extra for dusting
150g (5oz) caster sugar
100g (4oz) plain chocolate, chopped
1 large free-range egg, beaten
250ml (9fl oz) plain yogurt
2 tablespoons milk
75g (3oz) butter, melted
24 birthday candles to decorate

1 Preheat the oven to 190°C, 375°F, gas mark 5. Grease two 12-hole mini-muffin tin or line with paper cases.

2 Combine the flour, baking powder, cocoa and caster sugar and sift together into a large bowl, then add the chocolate.

3 In a separate bowl or jug, combine the egg, yogurt, milk and butter, then pour into the dry ingredients. Stir together until just combined, then spoon large dollops of the batter into the prepared muffin tin, making sure there are plenty of chocolate chunks peeping through the tops of the muffins.

4 Bake for about 20 minutes until risen and just firm.

5 Remove from the oven and leave to cool in the tin for a few minutes, before turning out onto a wire rack to cool completely.

6 To serve, dust with cocoa and stick a candle in the centre of each muffin.

Savoury Treats
& Breads

Four-seed Pesto Sensations

12 muffins

Scented with herby pesto and heaving with seeds, these wholesome-looking muffins are packed with healthy oils to keep you fighting fit and bouncing bright. Serve them as an accompaniment to a meal, or pop one in your lunchbox.

300g (10oz) plain flour
1 tablespoon baking powder
1 tablespoon caster sugar
½ teaspoon salt
2 tablespoons sesame seeds
2 tablespoons sunflower seeds
2 tablespoons pumpkin seeds
2 tablespoons poppy seeds
2 large free-range eggs, beaten
4 tablespoons olive oil
3 tablespoons pesto
300ml (10fl oz) milk
Ground black pepper

For the topping
2 teaspoons sesame seeds
2 teaspoons sunflower seeds
2 teaspoons pumpkin seeds
2 teaspoons poppy seeds

1 Preheat the oven to 200°C, 400°F, gas mark 6. Grease a 12-hole muffin tin or line with paper cases.

2 Combine the seeds for the topping in a bowl and set aside.

3 Combine the flour, baking powder, sugar and salt and sift into a large bowl, then sprinkle the seeds over the top.

4 In a separate bowl or jug, lightly beat together the eggs, olive oil, pesto and milk and add a grinding of black pepper. Pour into the dry ingredients and stir together until just combined.

5 Spoon large dollops of the batter into the prepared muffin tin, then sprinkle with the reserved topping seeds.

6 Bake for about 20 minutes until risen and golden.

7 Remove from the oven and leave to cool in the tin for a few minutes, before turning out onto a wire rack to cool completely.

Sun-dried Tomato & Oregano Muffins

12 muffins

Serve these muffins warm or cold topped with sprigs of fresh oregano, and lose yourself in those rich Mediterranean flavours. For extra indulgence, split open a warm muffin and fill with herby cream cheese.

300g (10oz) plain flour
1 tablespoon baking powder
½ teaspoon salt
3 tablespoons freshly grated
   Parmesan, plus extra for sprinkling
1 large free-range egg, beaten
250ml (9fl oz) milk
6 tablespoons olive oil
6 sun-dried tomatoes, roughly
   chopped, plus 1 extra for sprinkling
1 garlic clove, finely chopped
1 teaspoon fresh, chopped
   oregano
Ground black pepper

1 Preheat the oven to 190°C, 375°F, gas mark 5. Grease a 12-hole muffin tin or line with paper cases.

2 Combine the flour, baking powder and salt and sift into a large bowl, then sprinkle the Parmesan into the bowl.

3 In a separate bowl, lightly beat together the egg, milk and oil to combine, then stir in the tomatoes, garlic and oregano. Add a good grinding of black pepper, then pour into the dry ingredients and stir until just combined.

4 Spoon large dollops of the batter into the prepared muffin tin and sprinkle Parmesan and a few pieces of sun-dried tomato over each one, then grind over more black pepper.

5 Bake for about 20 minutes until risen and golden.

6 Remove from the oven and leave to cool in the tin for a few minutes, before turning out onto a wire rack to cool completely.

You could try other Mediterranean herbs such as basil or thyme too.

Roasted Pepper & Black Olive Muffins

12 muffins

Add a splash of colour to your muffin repertoire with these gorgeous cornmeal muffins. Chunks of sweet juicy pepper, shiny black olives and the bite of black pepper make these utterly moreish. They're fuss-free, too, if you use bottled roasted peppers – although you can roast your own, if you prefer.

200g (7oz) plain flour
100g (4oz) polenta
1 tablespoon baking powder
1 tablespoon caster sugar
½ teaspoon salt
175ml (6fl oz) buttermilk
2 large free-range eggs, beaten
100g (4oz) butter, melted
4 large pieces of bottled roasted
   pepper, chopped (about 125g
   (4½oz) each)
50g (2oz) pitted black olives, halved
Ground black pepper

1 Preheat the oven to 200°C, 400°F, gas mark 6. Grease a 12-hole muffin tin or line with paper cases or folded sheets of baking paper.

2 Combine the flour, polenta, baking powder, sugar and salt and sift into a large bowl.

3 In a separate bowl, combine the buttermilk, eggs and butter with about two-thirds of the roasted peppers and olives, and add a good grinding of black pepper. Pour into the dry ingredients and stir together until just combined.

4 Spoon large dollops of the batter into the prepared muffin tin. Press the remaining roasted peppers and olives into the tops of the muffins and grind over more black pepper.

5 Bake for about 20 minutes until risen and golden.

6 Remove from the oven and leave to cool in the tin for a few minutes, before turning out onto a wire rack to cool completely.

Smoked Salmon and Dill Muffins

Muffins probably aren't the most sophisticated baked treat known to mankind. But these ones made with smoked salmon and cream cheese are doing their best! Try serving them as a quirky savoury for afternoon tea – something of a mix between smoked salmon sandwiches and freshly baked scones.

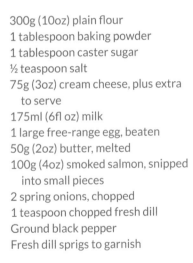

300g (10oz) plain flour
1 tablespoon baking powder
1 tablespoon caster sugar
½ teaspoon salt
75g (3oz) cream cheese, plus extra
    to serve
175ml (6fl oz) milk
1 large free-range egg, beaten
50g (2oz) butter, melted
100g (4oz) smoked salmon, snipped
    into small pieces
2 spring onions, chopped
1 teaspoon chopped fresh dill
Ground black pepper
Fresh dill sprigs to garnish

1 Preheat the oven to 200°C, 400°F, gas mark 6. Grease a 12-hole muffin tin or line with paper cases or folded baking paper.

2 Mix the flour, baking powder, sugar and salt and sift into a large bowl.

3 In a separate bowl, beat the cream cheese until soft, then gradually beat in the milk until smooth and creamy. Stir in the egg and butter, followed by the salmon, spring onions, dill and a good grinding of black pepper. Pour into the dry ingredients and stir until just combined, then spoon into the prepared muffin tin and grind over a little more black pepper.

4 Bake for about 20 minutes until risen and golden.

5 Remove from the oven and leave to cool in the tin for a few minutes, before turning out onto a wire rack to cool completely.

6 Serve spread with more cream cheese and dill sprigs to garnish.

Courgette, Feta & Spring Onion Cupcakes

12 cupcakes

The great chunks of feta in these cupcakes are a lovely surprise. The courgette adds moisture and flavour, as well as beautiful flecks of green. These go well with a spicy salsa. The batter is very stiff, almost dough-like, so don't worry and don't add more milk. The moisture in the courgette will loosen the texture.

250g (9oz) plain flour
2 tablespoons sugar
3 teaspoons baking powder
½ teaspoon salt
1 small courgette, grated
2 spring onions, finely chopped
250g (9oz) ricotta cheese
150g (5oz) feta cheese, crumbled
   into chunks
2 large free-range eggs,
   lightly beaten
50g (2oz) butter, melted
4 tablespoons milk

1 Preheat the oven to 200°C, 400°F, gas mark 6. Line a 12-hole muffin tin with paper cases.

2 Sift the flour, sugar, baking powder and salt into a large bowl, and mix through well. In another bowl, mix the courgette, spring onions, ricotta, feta, eggs, melted butter and the milk. Beat well, then add it to the dry ingredients. The batter will be stiff. Spoon it into the prepared cases.

3 Bake for about 20 minutes until risen and golden.

4 Remove from the oven and leave to cool in the tin for a few minutes, before turning out onto a wire rack to cool completely.

Perfect for picnics, lunchboxes or a summer lunch with friends.

Cheddar & Rosemary Bread

900g (2lb) loaf

This lovely loaf can be made freeform to have hunks torn off for lunch, or baked in a loaf tin for thin slices, buttered and quartered and presented nicely on a plate for afternoon tea. The herb doesn't have to be rosemary – thyme would also be great – and the cheese doesn't have to be Cheddar. Any hard cheese with plenty of flavour would be fine.

450g (1lb) strong white bread flour
1 teaspoon salt
1 teaspoon caster sugar
3 teaspoons English mustard powder
7g (¼ oz) dried yeast (to substitute
    fresh yeast, see page 216)
375ml (13fl oz) tepid water
2 teaspoons chopped fresh rosemary
400g (14oz) grated strong Cheddar
    cheese

1 In a large bowl, stir together the flour, salt, sugar, mustard powder and yeast, then add the water and mix until a dough forms. Tip the dough onto a well-floured work surface and knead for at least 10 minutes, until the dough is smooth and elastic. Form the dough into a ball and score a large, deep cross in the top. Put it back in the bowl, cover with a tea towel and leave somewhere warm to rise – this will probably take about 1 hour.

2 When the dough has doubled in size, knock out all the air and start kneading again, this time adding 250g (9oz) of the grated cheese in three batches. Just sprinkle a third over the dough and start kneading; when it has been incorporated, add the next third and so on. When all the cheese is incorporated, add the rosemary and knead the dough for another 5 minutes before either forming it into a loose shape and placing on a baking sheet, or putting it into a greased and floured 1kg (2¼lb) tin. Make lots of dimpled holes in the top of the loaf with your fingers, sprinkle any remaining cheese over the top and press in a bit more. Cover the dough with the tea towel and leave in a warm place to rise for another hour.

3 Preheat the oven to 190°C, 375°F, gas mark 5. The baking time depends on what shape you have made, but it will be about 20 minutes. You will know when it is done by tapping the bottom of the loaf. If it sounds hollow, it is ready. If you have cooked it in a tin, turn it out onto a wire rack to cool.

Beautiful Bread

There is nothing quite like the taste of a handmade, homemade loaf of bread fresh out of the oven. Breakfast, brunch, lunch or dinner, fresh bread is always a welcome addition to the table.

Basic white bread
450g (1lb) loaf

This is easy to make, does not require a bread machine, and gives the home baker a base from which to experiment.

400g (14oz) strong white bread flour
A large pinch of sea salt
15g (½oz) fresh yeast (to substitute dried yeast see page 216)
1 teaspoon sugar
200ml (7fl oz) warm water
1 medium free-range egg
100ml (3½fl oz) milk

1 Place the flour in a large bowl, add the salt and mix well. If using instant yeast, pour it over the flour. If using fresh yeast, mix together the yeast, sugar and warm water in a bowl. Leave in a warm place for 20 minutes until frothy.

2 Make a well in the centre of the flour and, using a wooden spoon, add the yeast mixture. Stir until you have a slightly wet paste. Tip this paste onto a well-floured surface then knead for 10–15 minutes, adding more flour if necessary, until the dough becomes firm and elastic and not sticky.

3 Put the dough into a floured mixing bowl, cover with a clean damp cloth and put it in a warm place such as an airing cupboard for 1 hour. Grease a 450g (1lb) loaf tin.

4 Remove the dough from the mixing bowl and place it on a lightly floured work surface. Form it into a sausage shape and put it into the prepared loaf tin. The dough should come two-thirds of the way up the inside of the tin.

5 Beat the egg and milk together, then paint the top of the dough with this egg wash. Allow to rise for 30–40 minutes until the dough comes above the top of the loaf tin.

6 Preheat the oven to 220°C, 425°F, gas mark 7. Brush the top of the dough again lightly with the eggwash and bake on a baking sheet for 10 minutes, then turn the oven down to 180°C, 350°F, gas mark 4 and bake for a further 20 minutes.

7 Tip the bread out and tap the sides and bottom of the loaf to check they sound hollow. Leave to cool on a wire rack for 1 hour before cutting.

Brewery bread with crystal malt

450g (1lb) loaf

By making bread using beer as both the liquid and the raising agent, you are creating something with a unique flavour. One of the most important ingredients in the production of British real ale is malted barley. Different strengths of malted barley produce different flavoured and different coloured beers. Sprinkle this delicious, crunchy malt over this bread just before it goes into the oven. The results are fantastic.

200g (7oz) strong wholemeal bread flour
225g (8oz) strong white bread flour
1 handful of crystal malt
1 tablespoon salt
20g (¾oz) fast-action dried yeast
2½ tablespoons butter, melted
300ml (10fl oz) good local beer
1 large free-range egg
Onion seeds
Sea salt

1 Mix all the dry ingredients except the onion seeds and sea salt together in a large bowl, then make a well in the centre and pour in the melted butter and beer. Stir to form a dough.

2 Tip the dough out onto a lightly floured work surface and knead for 10 minutes, then put it back into the bowl and leave it to rest in a warm place for 1 hour.

3 Return the dough to the lightly floured work surface and shape it into a ball, then flatten it and roll it up. Put the dough on a greased baking sheet and leave it to rise for a further hour.

4 Preheat the oven to 200°C, 400°F, gas mark 6. Beat the egg. Cut several slashes across the top of the bread and glaze with the egg. Sprinkle liberally with onion seeds and sea salt. Bake for 30 minutes, then transfer to a wire rack to cool.

Buttermilk oaten bread

2 × 225g (8oz) loaves

Fine oatmeal gives a wonderful gritty texture to this favourite Irish bread. Buttermilk was once a staple ingredient in breads and cakes, it gave a slightly sour taste and had good keeping qualities. Serve this as a satisfying part of 'high tea', warm with cheese or toasted with melting butter and thick fruity jams.

125g (4½oz) fine oatmeal
300ml (10fl oz) buttermilk
100ml (4fl oz) milk
225g (8oz) plain flour
1 teaspoon baking powder
¼ teaspoon salt

1 Soak the oatmeal in the buttermilk and milk overnight. The following day preheat the oven to 180°C, 350°F, gas mark 4. Grease a baking sheet.

2 Mix together the flour, baking powder and salt. Add the oatmeal and milk mixture and mix well to give a soft dough. Knead until smooth.

3 Divide into two portions and, on a lightly floured surface, roll each portion out to a thickness of about 2.5cm (1in) and about 10cm (4in) in diameter. Place both loaves on the prepared baking sheet and bake for 35–40 minutes until they are golden and sound hollow when tapped underneath. Remove from the oven and serve hot with butter.

Sesame rolls
14 rolls

The recipe for these little rolls comes from Trerice, an intimate Elizabethan manor house in Cornwall. They enjoy the sweet nuttiness of sesame and are delicious at teatime filled with smoked salmon or honey-roast ham. The glory of Trerice is the south-facing drawing room – a perfect room in which to take tea. Displayed there are some fine examples of Chinese porcelain tea bowls and little pots that were imported on the same ships that brought the chests of tea from the Orient.

15g (½oz) fresh yeast (to substitute dried yeast, see page 216)
2 teaspoons caster sugar
400ml (14fl oz) warm water
600g (1lb 5oz) strong white bread flour
1½ teaspoons full-cream milk powder (Coffeemate or similar)
½ teaspoon salt
25g (1oz) butter, softened
1 large free-range egg, beaten and mixed with a little water
2–3 tablespoons sesame seeds

1 Mix together the yeast, sugar and 6 tablespoons of the water. Leave in a warm place for 20–30 minutes until frothy.

2 Mix together the flour, milk powder and salt and rub in the butter. Add the yeast mixture and the remaining water and mix to a pliable dough. Knead until smooth and elastic, then place in a bowl, cover with a damp cloth and leave in a warm place for 1–1½ hours until doubled in size.

3 Grease two baking sheets. When the dough is well risen, divide into 60g (2½oz) pieces, form these into bun shapes and place on the prepared baking sheets. Brush the tops with egg wash and sprinkle liberally with sesame seeds. Leave in a warm place for about 30 minutes until well risen.

4 Preheat the oven to 200°C, 400°F, gas mark 6. Bake the rolls for 20–25 minutes until golden brown and firm. Remove from the oven and transfer to a wire rack to cool. Serve warm or cold.

5 As a variation, stir 1 tablespoon of sesame seeds into the dough with the yeast mixture. Sprinkle as above with more seeds before baking.

Historically, white bread was purely for the wealthy and was a status symbol. The bread that the peasants ate would have been coarse wholemeal, containing large amounts of husk and impurities.

Boxty bread
2 × 300g (10oz) loaves

Boxty bread is traditional festive Irish bread, flat and round and marked into four portions before baking to allow for easy division once cooked. With potatoes as its essentially Irish ingredient, it was once an indulgence for Shrove Tuesday, All Saints' Day or Hallowe'en.

225g (8oz) potatoes
225g (8oz) cooked and mashed
*   potatoes*
225g (8oz) plain flour
25g (1oz) butter, melted
Salt and ground black pepper

1 Preheat the oven to 190°C, 375°F, gas mark 5. Grease a baking sheet.

2 Wash and peel the raw potatoes. Grate into a clean cloth and wring well over a bowl to squeeze out the juice. Place the grated potatoes in a bowl with the mashed potatoes and mix together. Leave the starchy liquid in the bowl until the starch has settled, then pour off the liquid and add the starch to the potatoes. Add the flour, melted butter and seasoning and mix to a soft dough. Knead well.

3 Divide into two portions and, on a lightly floured surface, roll into flat circles. Place on the baking sheet and divide the top of each loaf into four with a sharp knife. Bake for around 40 minutes or until firm and golden. Remove from the oven and serve hot with butter.

Irish soda bread
450g (1lb) loaf

Soda bread is unique. Traditionally a poor-man's bread from Ireland, it has now attained something akin to cult status. Nothing quite compares to the nutty aroma of baking or cooling soda bread. It has great advantages for the modern cook over normal types of bread, in that it requires no rising. The basic principle, of course, is that it uses bicarbonate of soda and buttermilk in place of yeast. The most important thing to remember when making it is to do as little kneading as possible; the looser the dough, the better. Traditionally, the cross-shaped cut on top of the soda bread was made to bless the bread, and the corners were pricked to allow the fairies to escape.

400g (14oz) strong white bread flour
*   (to make brown soda bread, use half*
*   wholemeal flour and half strong white*
*   bread flour)*
1 teaspoon salt
1 teaspoon bicarbonate of soda
300–320ml (10–11fl oz) soured milk or
*   buttermilk to mix*

1 Preheat the oven to 230°F, 450°F, gas mark 8. Grease a baking sheet.

2 Sift the dry ingredients into a bowl. Make a well in the centre. Pour in most of the milk, then using one hand, mix in the flour from the sides of the bowl, adding more milk if necessary. The dough should be softish, not too wet and sticky.

3 When it all comes together, turn it out on to a well-floured work surface, then pat the dough into a circle about 4cm (1½in) thick. Put a cross on it and prick the corners. Put on the prepared baking sheet.

4 Bake for 15 minutes, then turn the oven down to 200°C, 400°F, gas mark 6 and bake for a further 30 minutes, or until cooked. If you are in doubt, tap the bottom of the bread – if it is cooked, it will sound hollow.

5 Remove from the oven and transfer to a wire rack to cool.

Organic wholemeal bread

2 x 900g (2lb) loaves

This lovely nutty-flavoured bread comes from Branscombe Bakery, the last traditional bakery to be used in Devon. Until 1987 it was run by brothers Gerald and Stuart Collier who baked bread, buns, cakes, tarts and scones every day of the year. The oven was lit at four o'clock every morning and then, three hours later when it had reached the required temperature, the ashes were raked out, the oven cleaned and the first batch of 130 loaves arranged inside.

Don't be tempted to cut into a freshly baked loaf if it has only just come out of the oven. Not only are you likely to burn your fingers, it will be difficult to cut. Wait until the loaf has cooled to a comfortable 'warm' temperature, which usually takes about half an hour.

25g (1 oz) organic fresh yeast (to substitute dried yeast, see page 216)
½ teaspoon light or dark soft brown sugar
600–750ml (1–1½ pints) warm water (it should be almost hand-hot, and the amount needed varies according to the flour used)
900g (2lb) organic wholemeal flour, warmed slightly in the oven
1 tablespoon sea salt
1 tablespoon corn or sunflower oil
1 tablespoon clear honey

1 Cream together the yeast and sugar and blend with 4–6 tablespoons of the warm water. Leave in a warm place for 10–20 minutes until frothy.

2 Mix together the flour and salt and make a well in the centre. Pour in the oil, honey, yeast mixture and enough of the remaining water to give a soft, elastic dough. Knead with the hands for about 10 minutes. Shape the dough into a ball and place in a lightly greased bowl. Dust the top with a little flour, cover with a clean damp cloth and leave in a warm, place until almost doubled in size (50 minutes to 2 hours).

3 Grease two 900g (2lb) loaf tins. Turn the dough out onto a lightly floured surface and knead vigorously for 8–10 minutes. Divide the dough into two equal portions and shape to fit the tins. Place in the tins, sprinkle the tops with a little more flour and cover with a clean damp cloth. Leave in a warm place for a further 30–40 minutes until the dough reaches the top of the tins.

4 Preheat the oven to 220°C, 425°F, gas mark 7. When the dough has risen, bake the loaves for 30 minutes. Remove from the oven and remove from the tins. Place the loaves in the oven for a further 10–15 minutes until they sound hollow when tapped. Remove from the oven and cool on a wire rack.

A Lighter *Bite*

Gooseberry Fool Cake

23cm (9in) cake

This gluten-free, gooseberry-laden sponge marries brilliantly with the light elderflower topping. Its high fruit content makes it a good source of vitamins. The cake is best made with the really tart, early season green gooseberries – red or yellow are sweeter – but frozen are fine if you can't get fresh. Keep the cake in the fridge and if the icing wilts after a day or two, re-fluff it with a fork.

150g (5oz) butter, melted, plus extra
    for brushing
Tapioca flour for dusting
5 large free-range eggs
200g (7oz) light soft brown sugar
200g (7oz) ground almonds
100g (4oz) sorghum flour
1½ teaspoons gluten-free baking
    powder
1½ teaspoons guar gum
1 teaspoon pure vanilla extract
A pinch of salt
450g (1lb) green gooseberries,
    topped, tailed, rinsed and dried

For the frosted berries
7 whole gooseberries, topped, tailed,
    rinsed and dried
1 small free-range egg white
1–2 tablespoons caster sugar

For the elderflower cream
200ml (7fl oz) double cream
2 tablespoons elderflower cordial
40g (1½oz) icing sugar, sifted

1 Preheat the oven to 180°C, 350°F, gas mark 4. Line a 23cm (9in) round springform cake tin with baking parchment, then brush with melted butter and dust with tapioca flour.

2 Crack the eggs into a large mixing bowl and beat with an electric mixer on high speed. Add the melted butter and beat again. Add the sugar, almonds, sorghum flour, baking powder, guar gum, vanilla and salt, then beat until creamy. Stir in the gooseberries using a rubber spatula. Be gentle: you want to keep the fruit intact as much as possible.

3 Spoon the batter into the prepared tin and bang the pan firmly on a work surface to get rid of air pockets. Bake for 45 minutes until firm and springy to the touch and a skewer inserted in the centre comes out clean.

4 Leave the cake to cool in the tin for 10–15 minutes. Cover a wire rack with baking parchment, then turn the cake out, right-way up, onto the rack. Leave to cool, then peel off the parchment.

5 Brush the gooseberries lightly with egg white, then roll them in caster sugar. Place the coated berries on a piece of baking parchment and leave to dry.

6 For the elderflower cream topping, whip the cream with the cordial and icing sugar until it forms stiff peaks. Spread the cream over the cake with a palette knife: make either peaks or create a smooth finish. Decorate with the frosted berries.

Raspberry Cake

20cm (8in) cake

This cake is gluten-free, simple to make and perfect for a summer's day. Once the topping is on, the cake should be quickly admired and then eaten before the cream slides off.

4 large free-range eggs
150g (5oz) light soft brown sugar
125g (4½oz) hazelnuts, ground
50g (2oz) polenta
25g (1oz) sorghum flour
1½ teaspoons gluten-free baking powder
1½ teaspoons guar gum
¼ teaspoon salt
75g (3oz) hazelnuts, toasted and chopped
150g (5oz) white chocolate, chopped
5–6 tablespoons raspberry jam
24 raspberries to decorate

For the roasted raspberries
200g (7oz) raspberries
4 tablespoons clear honey
½ teaspoon cinnamon sugar

For the cream filling & topping
200g (7oz) mascarpone
100ml (4fl oz) double cream
100ml (4fl oz) crème fraîche
75g (3oz) icing sugar
2 teaspoon lemon juice
1 teaspoon pure vanilla extract

For the raspberry sugar
1 freeze-dried raspberry
1 teaspoon icing sugar

1 Preheat the oven to 180°C, 350°F, gas mark 4. Brush two 20cm (8in) round sandwich tins with melted butter and dust with tapioca flour.

2 For the roasted raspberries, put the berries in a baking tin, drizzle with the honey and dredge with cinnamon sugar. Roast in the oven for 20 minutes. Leave to cool for 5 minutes.

3 Crack the eggs into a large bowl, then add the sugar, ground nuts, polenta, sorghum flour, baking powder, guar gum and salt. Beat well until creamy and stiff. Using a spatula, stir in the chopped nuts, white chocolate and roasted raspberries.

4 Divide the batter evenly between the prepared tins. Bake for 20–25 minutes until a skewer inserted in the centre comes out clean. Leave the cakes in the tins for a couple of minutes, then turn out onto a wire rack. Invert one so its flat bottom side is upwards.

5 For the cream filling, put the mascarpone, cream, crème fraîche, icing sugar, lemon juice and vanilla into a bowl and beat with an electric mixer until stiff.

6 For the raspberry sugar, use the back of a spoon to crush the freeze-dried raspberry to a fine powder. Sift in the 1 teaspoon icing sugar – if it is not pink enough, add a little more raspberry. Only mix little by little as you need it, as the freeze-dried raspberry goes soft after a couple of hours.

7 Spread one cake thickly with raspberry jam. Spread half the cream filling on top of the jam and place the second cake on top. Spread the remaining cream filling on top of the cake. Arrange the raspberries on top and dust the cake with raspberry sugar.

Upside-down Polenta Plum Cake

900g (2lb) cake

This is a great cake for using up any bumper seasonal fruit harvests, using plums, damsons, peaches or any fruit with a bit of body. The great thing about red-skinned plums is the gorgeous colour contrast against the sunshine-yellow polenta. When it is turned upside down, the lovely syrupy fruit juices seep into the sponge. Delicious served warm with homemade custard.

100g (4oz) butter, melted, plus extra, for brushing
2 large free-range eggs
185g (6½oz) polenta
75g (3oz) ground almonds
1½ teaspoons gluten-free baking powder
¾ teaspoon guar gum
¾ teaspoon pure vanilla extract
185g (6½oz) rice syrup
200g (7fl oz) crème fraîche
2 tablespoons orange juice

For the topping
8 red plums, halved and pitted
4 tablespoons light soft brown sugar
100ml (4fl oz) orange juice

1 Preheat the oven to 180°C, 350°F, gas mark 4. Brush a 900g (2lb) loaf tin with melted butter, line with baking parchment, then liberally butter the parchment.

2 First, make the topping. Put the plums, skin-side up, in a baking tin. Mix the brown sugar and orange juice and pour over the plums. Roast in the oven for about 15–17 minutes, until soft but still keeping their shape. Leave to cool in the tin.

3 Crack the eggs into a large bowl, then add the polenta, almonds, baking powder, guar gum and vanilla extract. In another bowl, mix the melted butter with the rice syrup, crème fraîche and orange juice. Beat with an electric mixer at low speed until just combined. Don't worry if it looks a bit curdled. Pour this mixture over the dry ingredients and beat at high speed until smooth and pale.

4 Take the plums out of the pan and put them in the loaf tin, skin-side down. Pour the syrup that remains in the baking tin into a measuring cup or jug and pour 4 teaspoons of the syrup over the plums in the loaf tin. Set the rest aside.

5 Spoon the cake batter into the loaf tin and spread it gently. Bake for 30 minutes, then cover with a disc of baking paper and bake for a further 15–20 minutes until springy to the touch and a skewer inserted in the centre comes out clean. As soon as the cake comes out of the oven, loosen the sides with a knife, then place a serving plate upside down on top of the tin and turn over quickly. Remove from the tin and peel off the baking paper. Spoon the remaining syrup from cooking the plums over the cake while it is still warm.

Custard Creams

Classic custard creams have been reinterpreted here in fabulous gluten-free form.

175g (6oz) butter, softened and
  cubed
175g (6oz) caster sugar
150g (5oz) polenta
150g (5oz) ground almonds
100g (4oz) custard powder
1 large free-range egg
½ teaspoon pure vanilla extract
Tapioca flour for dusting

For the filling
250g (9oz) butter, softened
100g (4oz) icing sugar, sifted
2 tablespoons custard powder
½ teaspoon pure vanilla extract

To decorate
1–2 tablespoons icing sugar, sifted
An icing bag fitted with a small
  star tube

1   Preheat the oven to 160°C, 325°F, gas mark 3. Line two large baking sheets with baking parchment.

2   Put the butter, sugar, polenta, almonds, custard powder, egg and vanilla into a large mixing bowl and beat using an electric mixer at low speed, until the mixture is combined and has formed a soft dough.

3   Dust your hands, rolling pin and work surface lightly with tapioca flour. Knead the dough gently and then roll out to about 5mm (¼in) thick. Using a pastry cutter (we used a 6cm (2½in) heart-shaped cutter), cut out the dough and place the shapes on the baking sheets. The biscuits will spread as they bake, so make sure you leave plenty of space between them.

4   Bake for 12–14 minutes, or until golden and firm to the touch (they will get firmer as they cool). Remove from the oven and leave to cool on the baking sheets for 5–10 minutes, before transferring to a wire rack to cool completely.

5   To make the filling, put the butter into a bowl. Sift the icing sugar and custard powder into the bowl, add the vanilla and beat using an electric mixer at medium speed until smooth. Chill in the fridge for 30 minutes.

6   Spoon the filling into an icing bag fitted with a small star tube. Turn half of the biscuits upside down and pipe the cream in swirls on top. Cover with the remaining biscuits – with the nice side facing upwards. To decorate, dust with icing sugar.

Cranberry, Pecan & Maple Syrup Flapjacks

These are generously laden with pecan nuts, and the maple syrup marries really well with both the nuts and the cranberries. It really is worth going to the effort of toasting the pecans.

Generous 175g (6oz) butter, softened, plus extra, melted, for brushing
100g (4oz) light soft brown sugar
3½ tablespoons golden syrup
3 tablespoons maple syrup
½ teaspoon salt
150g (5oz) gluten-free oats
100g (4oz) gluten-free oat flour
100g (4oz) pecan halves, toasted
50g (2oz) pecan halves, toasted and chopped
75g (3oz) millet flakes
75g (3oz) dried cranberries
Finely grated zest of 1 orange
½ teaspoon orange oil

For the topping
3 tablespoons dried cranberries
Finely grated zest of 1 orange
3 tablespoons maple syrup

1 Preheat the oven to 160°C, 325°F, gas mark 3. Line a 30 × 23 × 4cm (12 × 9 × 1½in) baking tin with baking parchment, then brush it liberally with melted butter.

2 Put the butter, sugar, golden syrup, maple syrup and salt into a pan and melt over a low heat, stirring every minute or so with a wooden spoon. Cook for 8–10 minutes until all the sugar has dissolved (when the bottom of the pan no longer feels gritty, the mixture is ready). Don't let the mixture boil or the flapjacks will be hard.

3 Put the oats, oat flour, halved and chopped pecan nuts, millet flakes, dried cranberries, orange zest and orange oil into a large bowl and stir. Pour in the melted butter mixture and stir well, using a rubber spatula. Ensure that all the dry ingredients are well coated.

4 Spoon the mixture into the tin and spread evenly, using a rubber spatula – you need to push it into the corners, but leave the surface fairly lumpy for a rustic effect. For the topping, scatter the cranberries over the surface, pressing them in lightly.

5 Bake for 15–17 minutes until golden with slightly darker edges. It will be bubbling and quite soft when you take it from the oven, but will firm up as it cools. Leave in the pan to cool for 10 minutes, then transfer to a wire rack to cool completely.

6 Mix the grated orange zest with the maple syrup and drizzle it over the flapjack while it is still warm. Cut into 15 slices.

Wholesome Treats

If you're looking for something nutritious but still delicious, here are some examples of healthier, satisfying snacks that will give you a nutrient boost but still feel like a treat – and won't break the calorie bank if you're watching your weight.

Bananas-a-go-go biscuits

12 biscuits

These tasty and filling biscuits are easy to make, are sugar- and wheat-free, the fat is 'healthy' fat, and they are really banana-y! They are soft biscuits, so don't wait for them to crisp up and they are best eaten on the day you make them.

3 ripe bananas
180g (6¼oz) pitted dates, chopped
175g (6oz) rolled jumbo oats
75ml (3fl oz) sunflower oil
1 teaspoon pure vanilla extract

1 Preheat the oven to 180°C, 350°F, gas mark 4 and line two baking sheets with baking parchment.

2 Mash the bananas in a large bowl, then add the dates, oats, sunflower oil and vanilla, and mix well. Leave the mixture to stand for 15–20 minutes to firm up a little and for the oats to absorb some of the liquid.

3 Drop teaspoons of the mixture onto the prepared baking sheets and flatten with the back of a spoon – they don't spread much, so the shape you make on the sheet will be the shape of the finished biscuit. Bake for 15–20 minutes until firm.

4 Remove from the oven and leave to cool for 5 minutes on the baking sheets before transferring to a wire rack to cool completely.

No-bake healthy humdingers

12 biscuits

This has got to be the ultimate in virtuous biscuits, as they have a lot of slow-release sugar properties and lots of natural ingredients. They make great sports snacks as well as being ideal for a mid-morning or mid-afternoon boost.

125g (4½oz) sunflower seeds
1 tablespoon tahini (sesame seed paste)
50g (2oz) desiccated coconut
1 tablespoon clear honey
40g (1½oz) wheatgerm
50g (2oz) dates, pitted and chopped

1 Bash the sunflower seeds a little in a mortar with a pestle or in a food processor. You just want to break them up a slightly. Tip them into a large bowl and add all the other ingredients.

2 Form the mixture into two rolls, wrap tightly in cling film and leave to chill in the refrigerator for 1-2 hours. When you are ready, just slice pieces off.

Maple cloud biscuits

12 biscuits

These biscuits have a light and fluffy texture – something between a soft cookie and a muffin. They are sugar-free, so are suitable for those who are sugar-intolerant, who often get ignored in the homemade biscuit department. Sugar substitutes can be found in supermarkets.

100g (4oz) butter, softened (although you could use something like a soy margarine)
100ml (4fl oz) soured cream
125g (4½oz) apple, peeled and grated
2 large free-range eggs
1 teaspoon maple syrup
½ teaspoon pure vanilla extract
250g (9oz) plain flour
65g (2½oz) granulated sugar substitute
1 teaspoon bicarbonate of soda
1 teaspoon baking powder

1 Preheat the oven to 190°C, 375°F, gas mark 5 and line two baking sheets with baking parchment.

2 Mix the butter, soured cream, apple, eggs, maple syrup and vanilla together in a large bowl. In another bowl, sift in the flour, sugar substitute, bicarbonate of soda and baking powder, then add the dry ingredients to the wet ingredients and mix very well. Drop dessertspoons of the mixture onto the prepared baking sheets and bake for about 10 minutes until pale golden. Transfer the biscuits to wire racks to cool.

Soft berry cookies
12 biscuits

These are just the most delicious, fruit-packed, oaty, soft cookies. They are easy to make and you can alter the fruit to whatever you can get your hands on. These are made with dried mangoes, raisins, figs, blueberries and pears – most dried soft fruits work beautifully.

60ml (2½fl oz) sunflower oil
75g (3oz) butter, softened
100g (4oz) light soft brown sugar
1 large free-range egg
½ teaspoon pure vanilla extract
100g (4oz) jumbo oats
150g (5oz) plain wholemeal flour
½ teaspoon bicarbonate of soda
½ teaspoon baking powder
½ teaspoon ground cinnamon
100g (4oz) dried apple
25g (1oz) cranberries
25g (1oz) blueberries

1 Preheat the oven to 180°C, 350°F, gas mark 4. Line two baking sheets with baking parchment.

2 Mix the sunflower oil, butter and sugar together in a large bowl. Beat in the egg and vanilla, then stir in the oats. Sift the flour, bicarbonate of soda, baking powder and cinnamon over the sugar and oil mixture and mix in. Add the dried fruit and stir until they are just combined.

3 Drop dessertspoonfuls of the mixture onto the prepared baking sheets, leaving lots of space between them because they spread, and bake for about 10 minutes until pale golden.

4 Remove from the oven and leave to cool for 5 minutes on the baking sheets before transferring to a wire rack to cool completely.

Chewy date biscuits
12 biscuits

Dates are just fantastic in cooking, and their intense sweetness means that you can reduce the amount of sugar you add to the recipe. These biscuits still contain sugar, as it's important for the chewy factor. You can reduce the amount of sugar you use, but it will change the overall consistency. You could also use entirely wholemeal flour instead of a mixture of white and brown. It is up to you.

75g (3oz) butter, softened
150g (5oz) light soft brown sugar
Finely grated zest of 1 large unwaxed lemon
1 large free-range egg
100g (4oz) plain flour
75g (3oz) wholemeal flour
1 teaspoon baking powder
½ teaspoon freshly grated nutmeg
1 teaspoon ground cinnamon
A pinch of salt
60ml (2½fl oz) milk
175g (6oz) pitted dates, chopped

1 Preheat the oven to 160°C, 325°F, gas mark 3. Line two baking sheets with baking parchment.

2 Cream the butter and sugar together in a large bowl until light and fluffy, then add the zest and egg and beat well. In another bowl, sift together the flours, baking powder, nutmeg, cinnamon and salt. Add to the creamed mixture in alternate dollops with the milk and beat well between each addition. Finally stir in the dates.

3 Drop round dessertspoonfuls of the mixture onto the prepared baking sheets, leaving space between them because they spread, and bake for 12–15 minutes until golden brown.

4 Remove from the oven and leave to cool for 5 minutes on the baking sheets before transferring to a wire rack to cool completely.

Peter Rabbit cookies

12 biscuits

Truly delicious little morsels, these carrot cookies contain both fruit and vegetables in one cookie, spiced with aromatic cinnamon.

200g (7oz) raw carrots, peeled and chopped
100g (4oz) hard white vegetable fat
100g (4oz) butter, softened
150g (5oz) light soft brown sugar
1 large free-range egg
300g (10oz) plain flour
1 teaspoon baking powder
1 teaspoon ground cinnamon
1 teaspoon ground ginger
75g (3oz) desiccated coconut
50g (2oz) crystallized papaya

1 Cook the carrots in a pan of unsalted boiling water until tender and then purée in a blender. You need to avoid any lumps, so push it through a sieve if you are unsure whether your purée is smooth enough. Leave to cool completely.

2 Preheat the oven to 200°C, 400°F, gas mark 6. Line two baking sheets with baking parchment.

3 Beat the white fat, butter and sugar together in a large bowl. You may need to scrape the white fat off the bowl every now and again, as it does like to stick to the sides. When the mixture is looking light and fluffy, add the egg and continue beating until everything is well amalgamated. Add the cold puréed carrots and mix in.

4 Sift the flour, baking powder, cinnamon and ginger onto the mixture and mix until incorporated. Finally mix in the coconut and papaya. Drop heaped teaspoons onto the prepared lined baking sheets, then flatten and press them into thinnish circles with the back of a spoon. Bake for about 10 minutes until golden, then transfer to a wire rack to cool.

Perfect in lunchboxes or to take to the office for a mid-morning nibble, these healthy cookies are also great for kids—they get fruit and vegetables all disguised as an indulgent treat.

Mildon flapjacks
12 biscuits

Flapjacks are just pushing the boundary of what is or what isn't a biscuit, but as you would eat them as you would a biscuit, so here they are. This is a recipe for a classic flapjack – still slightly chewy and moist. They are very comforting and the oats are amazingly good for you.

250g (9oz) butter
250g (9oz) caster sugar
175g (6oz) golden syrup
500g (1lb 2oz) jumbo oats

1 Preheat the oven to 180°C, 350°F, gas mark 4. Grease a 20cm (8in) square baking tin.

2 Melt the butter, sugar and golden syrup in a large pan. When melted, add the oats and stir until combined, then tip the mixture into the tin and press down firmly.

3 Bake for about 25 minutes until pale golden. It may look slightly undercooked and very soft, but it sets as it cools. The key is not to overcook the flapjack, as this way it remains chewy. When the flapjack comes out of the oven, quickly score it into pieces with a sharp knife and leave to cool in the tin.

These tasty treats also double up as a delicious offering for unexpected visitors. Keep a fresh batch handy in the biscuit tin.

Sweet
Somethings

Perfect Preserves

If you want to create the perfect afternoon tea, you'll need a selection of lovely fruit preserves. Making your own couldn't be more satisfying.

What is jam?

Jam is a mixture of fruit and sugar cooked together until set. Pectin, a gum-like substance that occurs in varying amounts in the cell walls of fruit, is essential to setting. Acid is also necessary to help release the pectin, improve the colour and flavour, and prevent crystallisation.

Fruits rich in pectin and acid are blackcurrants, cooking apples, crab apples, cranberries, damsons, gooseberries, lemons, limes, Seville oranges, quinces and redcurrants. Fruits containing a medium amount are dessert apples, apricots, bilberries, blackberries, greengages, loganberries, mulberries, plums and raspberries. Fruits low in pectin, which do not give a good set unless mixed with other high-pectin fruit, are cherries, elderberries, figs, grapes, japonica, medlars, nectarines, peaches, pears, rhubarb, rowanberries and strawberries. If acid is the only ingredient required and the fruit has enough pectin, the most convenient way of adding it is in the form of lemon, redcurrant or gooseberry juice.

To sterilise jars, bottles and lids

Wash in hot, soapy water or in the dishwasher, making sure that there is no residue on them, and then rinse thoroughly in hot water. Sterilise using one of the following methods:

Stand the jars or bottles and lids right-side up on a wire rack in a large pan, making sure that they do not touch each other or the sides of the pan. Cover completely with water and then bring to the boil. Reduce the heat and simmer for 10 minutes, then remove from the water and stand upside-down on a clean, thick cloth to drain. Dry completely in a preheated oven at 110°C, 225°F, gas mark ¼, right-side up, on a baking sheet for about 15 minutes. They can be kept warm in the oven until required.

Preheat the oven to 180°C, 350°F, gas mark 4. Stand the jars, bottles and lids on the oven shelf and leave for 10 minutes to sterilise. Turn the oven off and keep them warm until you are ready to fill the jars with jam.

If your dishwasher has a very hot cycle, you can sterilise your jars, bottles and lids in that.

To make jam

Choosing and preparing the fruit

- Fruit should be dry, fresh and barely ripe. Over-ripe fruit does not set well, as it is low in pectin.
- Pick over the fruit, discarding any damaged parts, and wash or wipe it.
- Simmer gently until soft and reduced by about one-third to break down the cell walls and release the pectin. Make sure that all fruit skins are completely soft, especially thick-skinned fruits such as blackcurrants, before adding the sugar, because this will instantly toughen them.

Choosing and using the sugar

- Any kind of sugar (except icing sugar) will make jam, but preserving sugar makes a slightly clearer jam which needs less stirring, and produces far less scum. Brown sugars can mask the fruit flavour.
- Commercial jam sugar, based on granulated sugar with added pectin and acid, guarantees a set for any fruit. Choose the type that guarantees a set in 4 minutes with no testing. This is useful for low-pectin fruits but is rather expensive.
- Warm the sugar in the oven before adding it to the fruit to reduce the cooking time. Take the pan off the heat before adding the sugar and stir until completely dissolved.

If the mixture boils before the sugar is dissolved, it will crystallise and the jam will be crunchy and spoilt. Once the sugar has dissolved completely, bring the jam to a rolling boil (the boiling will continue when the jam is stirred with a wooden spoon).

Testing for a set

Most jams reach setting point after 5–20 minutes' boiling, but you should always start testing for a set after 5 minutes as over-boiling spoils the colour and flavour.

Saucer Test

Before you start making your jam, put a saucer into the fridge or freezer to get cold. Remove the jam from the heat and put about 2 teaspoons onto the cold saucer. Allow it to cool, then push your fingertip across the centre of the jam. If the surface wrinkles well and the two halves remain separate, setting point has been reached. If not, return the pan to the heat and boil again for 5 minutes, then test again.

Temperature Test

If you have a sugar thermometer, hold it in the boiling jam, without resting it on the bottom of the pan. Bend over until your eyes are level with the 105°C (220°F) mark on the thermometer: this is the temperature the jam should reach when it is at setting point.

Flake Test

To check the setting point, do a quick 'flake' test. Dip the bowl of a cold wooden spoon into the jam. Take out and cool slightly, then let the jam drop from the edge of the spoon. At setting point, the jam runs together, forming flakes, which break off cleanly with a shake of the spoon.

Potting and covering

- Wash the jars in very hot water and dry in the oven at 140°C, 275°F, gas mark 1. Leave them there until you are ready to pot the jam. The jars must be warmed before filling, or the hot jam will crack them.
- Once the setting point has been reached, pot the jam immediately, except for strawberry and raspberry jam and all marmalades. Leave these to stand for 10–15 minutes to let the fruit or rind settle, to prevent it from rising to the surface in the jar.
- Use a jam funnel and a ladle or a small jug to fill the jars almost to the top. This ensures there is no space for bacteria to grow.
- Cover the jam immediately with waxed paper discs, placing the waxed sides down on the surface of the preserve. The surface of the jam should be completely covered by the waxed paper (buy the right size for the type of jar used). Press gently to

exclude all air. Immediately put on the lids or fix dampened cellophane covers (damp-side downwards) and secure with rubber bands.

- For every 1.35kg (3lb) sugar, the yield will be about 2.25kg (5lb) jam.

Storing

- Stand the jars of jam aside until completely cold, then label them clearly with type of jam and the date it was made.
- Store in a cool, dark, dry and airy cupboard. Homemade jam will keep well for up to one year, but may deteriorate in colour and flavour if kept longer.

Strawberry jam
2.5kg (5lb 10oz) jam

This is the jam everyone loves, young and old, and is the traditional one served with National Trust cream teas. It is only worth making if you have a good supply of fresh fruit from your own garden, or direct from a pick-your-own farm. This recipe will take several days, although it is very simple. Strawberries are lacking in acid and pectin, so choose small, firm berries, preferably of the more acid varieties, and use jam sugar to ensure a good set. If you have problems getting the jam to set, add the juice of 1 lemon when bringing the fruit and sugar to the boil.

1.5kg (3lb 5oz) small strawberries
1.5kg (3lb 5oz) jam sugar

1 Hull the strawberries, but do not wash them, and then layer with two-thirds of the sugar in a wide, shallow china or glass bowl. Sprinkle over the remaining sugar. Cover with a clean cloth and leave at room temperature (as long as your room is not too warm) for 24 hours.

2 Next day, scrape the contents of the bowl into a pan and bring slowly to the boil. Allow the mixture to bubble over a low heat for 5 minutes and then remove from the heat, cover with a clean cloth and leave for a further 48 hours.

3 Return the pan to the heat and bring back to the boil. Boil for about 10–15 minutes until setting point is reached (see page 197). Remove the pan from the heat and skim off any scum. Allow the jam to cool for 10 minutes and then give it a good stir, so that the fruit is well dispersed – it will then remain suspended rather than rising to the top of the jam. Pot and cover in the usual way.

Apricot jam
2.25kg (5lb 8oz) jam

Apricots need extra acid to give a good set, so lemon juice is added. This jam is especially good with freshly baked croissants.

1.35kg (3lb) fresh apricots
Juice of 1 lemon, strained
300ml (10fl oz) water
1.35kg (3lb) granulated sugar, warmed

1 Halve and stone the apricots, reserving 12 stones. Using a nutcracker, crack open the stones and remove the kernels. Blanch them in boiling water for 1 minute, then drain and transfer to a bowl of cold water. Drain again, then rub off the skins with your fingers.

2 Simmer the apricots and kernels gently in the lemon juice and water for about 15 minutes, or until the fruit is soft and the water has reduced. Add the warmed sugar and stir until it has completely dissolved, then boil rapidly for 10–15 minutes, or until setting point is reached (see page 197). Pot and cover in the usual way.

Raspberry jam
2kg (4lb 8oz) jam

You need slightly under-ripe raspberries to make really successful jam with no hint of mustiness or mould, so if you do not grow your own raspberries, the next best thing is to find a pick-your-own farm. Loganberries can be used instead.

1kg (2¼lb) raspberries
1kg (2¼lb) granulated sugar

1 Pick over the raspberries carefully, but do not wash them. Put them in a large, shallow china or glass dish and pour over the sugar. Cover with a clean cloth and leave for 24 hours, pounding them together every now and again.

2 Next day, tip the raspberry and sugar mixture into a pan and bring very slowly to the boil, stirring frequently. Boil fast for 3–5 minutes, or until setting point is reached (see page 197). Pot and cover in the usual way.

High dumpsie dearie jam
4.5kg (10lb) jam

Although an old Gloucestershire recipe, this jam was popular all over England in Victorian times, when it was called 'Mock Apricot Jam'.

900g (2lb) cooking apples, peeled
  and cored
900g (2lb) cooking pears, peeled
  and cored
900g (2lb) large plums
Juice of 1 large lemon, strained
300ml (10fl oz) water
3 whole cloves
1 small cinnamon stick
2.75kg (6lb) granulated sugar, warmed

1 Cut the apples and pears into even-sized pieces. Halve and stone the plums, reserving the stones, then place all the fruit in a large pan with the lemon juice and water. Tie the reserved plum stones, cloves and cinnamon in a piece of muslin and add to the fruit. Simmer very gently until the fruit is soft.

2 Remove and discard the muslin bag. Add the warmed sugar and stir until it has completely dissolved, then bring to the boil. Boil rapidly for about 15 minutes until setting point is reached (see page 197). Pot and cover in the usual way.

Cliveden red gooseberry & elderflower jam

2.25kg (5lb) jam

This recipe was created by the cooks at Cliveden's Conservatory Restaurant, just outside Maidenhead. Omit the elderflowers, if you wish, and substitute scented geranium leaves or other herbs.

1.35kg (3lb) gooseberries
300ml (10fl oz) water
6–8 elderflower heads
1.35kg (3lb) granulated sugar, warmed

1 Place the gooseberries in a large pan and add the water. Simmer the fruit gently for about 20 minutes, or until pulpy. Meanwhile, snip the tiny flowers off the elderflower heads, making sure they are clean and insect-free.

2 Stir the flowers and warmed sugar into the cooked fruit. Heat gently, stirring until the sugar has dissolved, and then boil rapidly for about 15 minutes until setting point is reached (see page 197). Pot and cover in the usual way.

Variations

Gooseberry & orange jam
Cook the gooseberries with the grated zest and juice of 3 oranges instead of the elderflowers.

Gooseberry & redcurrant jam
Use 900g (2lb) gooseberries and 450g (1lb) redcurrants and omit the elderflowers.

Gooseberry & rhubarb jam
Use 900g (2lb) gooseberries and 450g (1lb) chopped rhubarb. Cook the fruits separately to avoid overcooking the rhubarb. Omit the elderflowers.

Gooseberry & strawberry jam
Use 750g (1½lb) gooseberries and 750g (1½lb) strawberries. Cook the fruits separately to avoid overcooking the strawberries. Omit the elderflowers.

Greengage & orange jam
1.8kg (4lb) jam

Adding orange works very well with the subtle flavour of greengage jam.

900g (2lb) greengages
1 large orange
½ lemon
900g (2lb) granulated sugar, warmed

1 Wash the fruit and remove the stones, but reserve them. Put the fruit in a pan and tie the stones in a square of muslin. Add the muslin bag to the pan with the juice and thinly pared and sliced rind of the orange and lemon. Simmer gently for about 10 minutes, or until the greengages are soft.

2 Stir in the warmed sugar and continue simmering gently, stirring continuously until the sugar has dissolved, then bring to a rolling boil. Boil for about 10 minutes until setting point is reached (see page 197). Remove from the heat and squeeze the muslin bag. Open it and crack some of the stones with a nutcracker; remove the kernels. Stir these kernels into the jam and then pot and cover in the usual way.

For Greengage, Orange and Walnut Jam, stir in a generous handful of chopped walnuts after setting point is reached.

Blackcurrant jam
2.25kg (5lb) jam

Blackcurrants make a gorgeously rich jam with a wonderful flavour, but make sure the initial cooking is thorough so that the skins are soft. Taste every now and again to check that the currants are well cooked before you add the sugar.

900g (2lb) blackcurrants
600ml (1 pint) water
1.35kg (3lb) granulated sugar, warmed

1 Wash the currants and remove the strings and stalks. Place in a pan with the water and bring slowly to the boil. Reduce the heat and simmer gently for about 20 minutes, or until the fruit is tender, stirring occasionally.

2 Add the warmed sugar to the pan, stir until completely dissolved and then boil rapidly for about 5 minutes or until setting point is reached (see page 197). Pot and cover in the usual way.

Rhubarb & rose-petal jam
750g (1lb 10oz) jam

Use freshly picked, unsprayed, scented rose petals, red if possible, from the garden. Do not buy roses from a florist, as they will have been sprayed. Red roses give a better flavour and a lovely colour.

450g (1lb) rhubarb
Juice of 1 lemon
450g (1lb) granulated sugar
2 handfuls of scented rose petals
    (about 5 roses)

1 Wipe the rhubarb and cut into 1cm (½in) pieces. Put in a shallow china dish, add the lemon juice and then cover the rhubarb with the sugar. Cover with a clean cloth and leave to stand overnight.

2 Next day, remove the white, or heel, from each rose petal and discard. Cut the rose petals into strips and put in a pan with the rhubarb mixture. Bring to the boil slowly, stirring until the sugar has dissolved. Boil briskly until setting point is reached (see page 197). Leave to cool slightly and then pot and cover in the usual way.

Variations

Blackcurrant & rhubarb jam
Cook 450g (1lb) rhubarb in 300ml (10fl oz) water until pulpy. In another pan cook 450g (1lb) blackcurrants until tender. Mix the two fruits together and continue as for Blackcurrant Jam.

Blackcurrant & apple jam
Cook 350g (12oz) peeled, cored and sliced apples in 300ml (10fl oz) water until tender. Add to the cooked blackcurrants and continue as for Blackcurrant Jam.

Tips &
Techniques

Successful Baking

Some of the most important keys to successful baking are using good-quality ingredients, the correct oven temperature and careful cake tin preparation. Follow the advice below and you'll be well on your way to creating afternoon tea delights worthy of any National Trust tea room.

The Right Ingredients

Flour

- Plain flour is generally used when little rise is required; for example, in pastries and shortbreads. To convert plain flour to self-raising flour, add baking powder in the quantities that are recommended on the container for different types of baking.
- Self-raising flour is used for cakes that need a raising agent. In some recipes, however, the amount of raising agent already added to the flour may be too great. In that case, either plain flour with a raising agent, or a mixture of plain and self-raising flour is used.
- Always store flour in a cool, dry place, preferably in an airtight container. If you wish, you can sift the flour to remove any lumps and to incorporate extra air before adding the flour to the cake mixture.

Raising agents

- Baking powder is the most commonly used raising agent. It gives off carbon dioxide, which forms bubbles in the batter. These expand during cooking, making the cake, scone or biscuit rise and helping to produce a light texture. Too much baking powder can cause heaviness.
- Bicarbonate of soda is often used in recipes that include soured milk or buttermilk, spices, black treacle and honey.
- Soured milk is sometimes used to give extra rise to heavy mixtures. It can be made by leaving milk in a warm place until it curdles.
- Buttermilk is a standard ingredient in both Welsh and Irish cookery.
- Yeast was once the only raising agent available for home baking, but it is now generally used only in bread-making and in some traditional fruit or spice breads or pastries, such as Suffolk Fourses, Chelsea Buns and Lardy Cake.

Dried yeast keeps for several months in an airtight container. Fresh yeast lasts for about a week in the fridge and will freeze for up to six months. Fresh yeast is often available from large supermarkets with bakeries, or from local bakers. You may have to ask for it as it is not a 'shelf' item, but it is sometimes free of charge. Dried or fast-action yeast can be substituted for fresh yeast. For 10g (½oz) fresh yeast use 5g (¼oz) dried or fast-action yeast; for 25g (1oz) fresh yeast use 10g (½oz) dried or fast-action yeast; and for 60g (2oz) fresh yeast use 20g (¾oz) dried or fast-action yeast. If using dried yeast, dissolve it in a little liquid of the recipe and leave it to froth in a warm place for 15 minutes before adding to the other ingredients. If using fast-action yeast, add it to the dry ingredients before mixing in the other ingredients. If using dried or fast-action yeast, the dough only needs to rise once.

Fats

- Butter and margarine are interchangeable in most recipes, but butter is better in shortbreads and rich fruit cakes that are going to be stored for some time and matured.
- Lard or white vegetable fat is often used in biscuits and cookies and gives a shorter texture.
- Oil is excellent in carrot cakes and chocolate cakes.
- Allow butter, margarine or shortening to soften to room temperature for at least an hour before using. Soft or whipped margarines can be used straight from the fridge.

Eggs

- Eggs should be at room temperature; if taken straight from the fridge they are more likely to curdle.
- Small eggs are too small for most recipes. Use large or medium, depending on what the recipe specifies.

Sugar

- Caster sugar is generally used for creamed mixtures as it gives a much lighter texture than other types of sugar.
- Granulated sugar is acceptable in rubbed-in mixtures, but it can produce a slightly gritty texture. It is worth paying a little extra for caster sugar.
- Soft brown sugar gives a caramel flavour and beats well in creamed mixtures. The darker variety has a stronger flavour.
- Demerara sugar is very good in teabreads and in mixtures where ingredients are melted together, such as gingerbreads and boiled fruit cakes. It is excellent for sprinkling on the top of loaves and biscuits.
- Black treacle has a dark colour and strong flavour and is often used in gingerbreads.
- Golden syrup gives a soft, moist, sometimes sticky texture, which is perfectly suited to gingerbreads and flapjacks.
- Honey adds a very distinctive flavour but too much will cause the batter to burn easily.

Lining pie dishes and plates

Roll out the pastry to a thickness of 3–5mm (⅛–¼in) and a little larger in size than the prepared dish or plate. Lay the pastry carefully on the dish, making sure that no air is trapped underneath. Do not stretch the pastry as it will only shrink back.

If it is not large enough, roll out a little more and try again. Ease the pastry into all the rims and corners of the dish, then trim off any surplus. (Trimmings may be useful to make crosses on hot cross buns or a trellis over the top of a tart or pie.)

Preparing tins

Most non-stick cake tins are very reliable if you follow the manufacturers' instructions but, to be on the safe side, it is wise to grease and line them anyway. Grease tins with whatever fat or oil is to be used in the recipe, then line with non-stick baking paper. Cut a single piece for the bottom of the pan and, when fitting paper to the sides, cut into the corners to make quite sure that the paper lies neatly against the tin. It may also be necessary to cut and overlap the paper, as the sides of circular pans sometimes slope slightly.

Oven temperatures

Always make sure that the oven has reached the correct temperature before putting in the item to be baked. If you are not sure whether your oven temperature gauge is accurate, buy an oven thermometer and make regular checks. If you are using a convection (fan-assisted) oven, reduce all recommended temperatures by 20°C, 68°F.

Is it ready?

To see if a sponge cake is ready, press the centre lightly with a finger; if it springs back, it is cooked. To test fruitcakes and gingerbreads, stick a flat cake skewer into the centre of the cake and withdraw it immediately. If the skewer comes out clean, the cake is done. If not, allow a further 5 minutes and test again. Biscuits are usually ready when they are just turning golden. Scones are firm, well risen and golden. If a cake begins to darken too quickly, place a double or triple layer of baking paper over the top and continue cooking as usual.

Crumple your baking paper and open out again to make it easier to place in your tin.

Pastry know-how

The aim is to make pastry as light as possible, and this depends on how much cold air is trapped in the dough before baking. The secret is to use cold ingredients, to have cold hands, cold bowls, a cold slab or surface on which to roll (marble is ideal) and to work in a cool room. Work quickly and lightly, using the fingertips when rubbing in, as too much handling will make the pastry tough. When rolling, sprinkle just a little flour on the work surface and use light, even movements.

Most pastry recipes call for plain flour, but self-raising is sometimes used for suet crust and shortcrust. The more fat that is used, the shorter the pastry will be; if the amount of fat is less than half the amount of flour, add 1 teaspoon baking powder for each 225g (8oz) of flour. Butter, or butter mixed with lard, is best. Rich pastry needs a hotter oven than others. If the oven is too cool, the fat will run out of the pastry and the pastry will be tough and chewy.

Golden rules

Always use the right tin for the recipe. Smaller or larger tins will affect the cooking time and hence the texture of the finished cakes.

Except in fan-assisted ovens, most cakes and biscuits cook best in the centre of the oven. Rich fruit cakes, large cakes and shortbreads should be placed just below the centre, and small, plain cakes, Swiss rolls and scones just above.

Do not disturb the cake during the first three-quarters of the baking time or, better still, not until you think it may be ready. Draughts or knocks can make the cake sink.

When placing biscuits on prepared baking sheets, always allow room for them to spread during baking. It is better to leave too much room than to have all the biscuits merging into one misshapen mass.

Baking blind

This is necessary when an uncooked filling is to be put into the pastry case, or to set the pastry before any filling is poured in and cooked. When the prepared tin has been greased and lined with the pastry, prick the base all over with a fork. Cover the base with a piece of baking paper followed by a layer of baking beans (available in any good cook shop) or dried pasta or pulses (dried haricot beans, dried kidney beans or chickpeas). Bake in a preheated oven for just under the required time, then remove from the oven, lift out the baking beans and the baking paper and bake for 5 minutes more to dry out the base.

Notes on the recipes

Follow one set of measurements only. Eggs are large and preferably free-range.

Spoon measurements are level. 1 teaspoon = 5ml; 1 tablespoon = 15 ml.

Most recipes need a little extra butter or other oil for greasing tins.

Pastry and other rolled recipes need a little extra flour for dusting.

Top Tips

Oven temperatures vary considerably, so you need to use your judgement when deciding on the temperature to set your oven and the time the item will take to cook. Even if we all had the same make and model of oven, they would all cook slightly differently. So use the temperature indicated in the recipe, but be prepared to adjust it if you seem to consistently need a lower or higher temperature. Similarly, you may need to adjust cooking times.

Because all ovens vary, there is an element of using your own judgement in baking as well as just following a recipe. Have a look at the cake at least 5 minutes before the end of the allotted cooking time and see whether it's time to a) retrieve it; b) cover it with a double sheet of baking paper to prevent the top burning and give it another 10 minutes; or c) just leave it for another 5 minutes. You'll soon learn to get used to your own oven.

A cake is generally done when a sharp knife or flat cake skewer inserted in the centre comes out clean without any raw cake batter sticking to it. The cake should be firm to the touch and, in the case of a sponge, have a bit of a spring to it when you give it a gentle press. It should not feel rock hard or too spongy soft. It may also have started to pull away from the side of the tin.

If you have followed all the instructions and something has still gone wrong, you'll find some troubleshooting tips on page 213 to rescue the cake and also to help you prevent the same thing from happening again.

Never admit that the cake you present with a flourish is not what you had first envisaged. You can disguise most problems and no one need ever know.

Cakes are done if they are firm to the touch and a bit springy on top. You can also insert a skewer into the centre – if it comes out clean, the cake is done.

Oven tips

Always use your common sense when you are baking. Every oven is different and has its own special foibles. Some ovens cook slightly quicker, some slightly slower. Some ovens have 'hot patches' so you'll need to turn the sheet to prevent half your cakes or biscuits browning more than the other half. Make a mental note of your oven's particular quirks and you will be able to pre-empt any disasters.

Muffin tips

You could pretend there's a huge amount of skill and talent involved in baking a batch of golden-brown, sweetly scented muffins – but I'm afraid that's not strictly true. They are so unbelievably easy to make, anyone can do it – even self-professed failures in the kitchen. But there are a few secrets to making really light fluffy muffins that differ from cakes and biscuits – see in particular point three below (which may well appeal directly to the more slapdash cooks among us).

Number 1: To make a sweeping generalisation – combine your dry ingredients, combine your wet ingredients, put the two together and bingo: 12 muffins! But before you get to this stage, there's a golden rule ...

Number 2: Even if this seems like a nuisance, do it anyway! Sift all your dry ingredients together before you add the wet ingredients. You want your flour, sugar, cocoa, etc. to be as light as air, filling your mixing bowl in soft drifts ready to combine with the wet ingredients.

Number 3: Once you add the wet ingredients, don't over-mix. The temptation is to give the batter a thorough beating to get it lovely and smooth. However, this is counter-productive and will result in a denser, heavier muffin. Give it a gentle, brief stir – just enough to combine the ingredients. Your muffin batter will normally still look a bit lumpy and chunky, and it's fine to still have a few streaks of flour. Just scoop up large spoonfuls of the batter, dollop them into the cases, then pop the tin in the oven. Twenty minutes later you'll be in heaven and wondering why you don't make these gorgeous creations every morning.

And if you don't follow this advice? Well, they'll still be edible, but your muffins won't have that fabulously fluffy texture that all the best muffins should have. They'll be a little tough, a little bit more solid than you'd like. So always give your muffins the quick 1-2-3 treatment.

Batches of biscuits

All the biscuit recipes give you a rough indication of how many biscuits they will make, although it is tempting – and rather more accurate in a way – to say they all make 'one batch'.

By that, it means you shouldn't have so few as to make it not worthwhile and you shouldn't have too many so that you are eating them for weeks. The actual number, however, will vary and, in fact, is not particularly relevant.

If you roll your dough slightly more thinly, you'll get more biscuits, for example, or slightly fewer if you roll it more thickly. You may use a small heart-shaped cutter or an large rectangle, in which case the difference in number will be even more. Different people's idea of rolling a golf-ball-sized ball of dough may vary considerably.

The point is that it really doesn't matter. If the texture of your dough is correct, you'll have great biscuits – however many there are.

Melting chocolate

There are two methods of melting chocolate.

The first is the safest method. Place the chopped-up chocolate in a heatproof bowl over a pan of barely simmering water. The crucial thing here is that the bottom of the bowl must not touch the water otherwise the chocolate gets too hot. If that happens, it will spoil and go grainy.

If it does seem to be going grainy, remove the bowl from the heat immediately, stand it in a bowl of very cold water and stir vigorously. If you have acted quickly enough, you may rescue it. If not, you will have to throw it away.

The second method is quicker but not without risk: the microwave. Put the chopped chocolate into a microwaveable container, then heat in short bursts of 10–15 seconds, stirring each time. Stop while there are still some lumps and keep stirring – the residual heat will melt the rest.

The danger here is that it can turn in a matter of seconds from melting beautifully to burning. Again, if you are quick enough, you may be able to rescue it by cooling it, but otherwise the only solution in that case is to start again.

Most types of biscuit dough freeze well for up to a month if you wrap them carefully in baking paper and cling film, so if a recipe makes what looks like too much, simply freeze half for another occasion.

Troubleshooting Tips

If your cake is solid and brick-like, there are a couple of things that may have gone wrong: you may not have beaten enough air into the batter – in which case an electric mixer is better than a wooden spoon – or if the recipe required you to fold in the flour, you may have been a bit too vigorous and beaten all of the air out of your batter – next time use a large metal spoon and fold gently in a figure-of-eight motion.

With a cake that has risen unevenly, just level the top, turn it upside down and ice the bottom.

If your cake is a bit dry and crumbly, the batter might have been too stiff and dry and the oven temperature may have been a little high. Next time, lower the oven temperature and add a splash of milk to the batter.

A cake may have sunk in the centre for a couple of reasons: there may have been too much raising agent, or too soft a batter. Check the oven temperature, too. An oven that is too hot or too cool can cause a cake to sink.

If the fruit sinks to the bottom of your cake, it's generally because the mixture is too soft or sticky to carry the fruit as it rises. Rinse and dry glacé cherries or other fruit and check your mix is not too runny.

Don't throw out a cake because of its texture. If it is inedible as a cake, make it into cake crumbs and freeze them – there are lots of uses for cake crumbs in other recipes and it's handy to have a stash tucked away. If the cake is flat, use a cutter to cut out shapes and sandwich them together with jam or buttercream.

A cake with a massively sunken centre can be turned into a delicious pudding; cut out the centre and pile whipped cream and fruit into the hole. A dusting of icing sugar, and voilà, a show-stopping dessert!

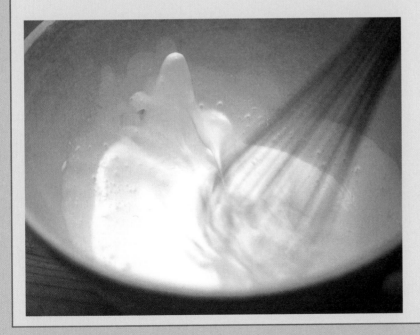

Using the Icing Bag

Many people are put off using an icing bag because it looks a bit tricky. The key is to practise first on a plate until you get the feel for it and are able to control the flow of icing from the tube. Once you can do that, you're well on your way to professional-looking cakes, cupcakes and biscuits – and you'll be able to use your new-found skills with both buttercream and royal icing.

Choosing nozzles

The piping tubes for the icing bag are the metal or plastic cone-shaped pieces that you place inside the icing bag. The icing is squeezed through the nozzle, thus creating different effects, depending on the size and pattern on the tube.

Start with a small plain round end and practise simple lines and dots with royal icing. Then you can experiment with the different patterns made with different tubes.

For buttercream, use a star-shaped tube at first to practise swirls. These are particularly effective on cupcakes!

Decorating with royal icing

Royal icing is great for adding details to cakes, biscuits and cupcakes. It is also very simple to mix with colouring gels so it can be used to add little splashes of colour to an otherwise plain treat.

Dots

The consistency of your royal icing is crucial – too stiff and your dots will be awkward-shaped peaks; too runny and your lines will disappear into the background. Experiment until you get it just right, and only then make a start on your cakes.

Hold the bag comfortably in your writing hand, moving it around until you feel in control of the tube. Practise dots first on a plate or piece of card. Hold the decorating bag so the tube is just slightly above and perpendicular to the surface to be decorated. In one smooth movement, squeeze the bag so the icing pools around the tube, release the pressure on the bag and then pull the tube upwards and away from the dot. The dot should settle to form a perfect dome. If it still has a peak after a couple of minutes, your royal icing is too stiff.

Lines

To create lines, hold the icing bag in the same way as for dots, but angle the tip at about 45 degrees to the surface you are decorating. Touch the tip of the tube to the surface, then start squeezing the icing bag at the same time as you start moving the tube slowly across the surface. Ensure you keep the tube moving at the same rate as the flow of royal icing for a smooth line – too fast and you will break the line; too slow and you will get an uneven width. To finish a line neatly, touch the tip of the tube to the surface, release the pressure on the bag and bring the tube up and away from the surface, much the same as piping dots.

Try twisting the tube and bag slightly as you work for an even swirlier swirl!

Decorating with buttercream

Buttercream is so simple to make, and if you go the extra mile and apply it with an icing bag you'll be rewarded with professional, beautiful results. You can then use sprinkles, sugar decorations, chocolate chips – anything edible and pretty to enhance your buttercream topping. Or you can leave it plain and let the swirls steal the show.

Swirls

Choose a star-shaped, reasonably large tube, about 1cm (½in) in diameter. It's great to use a saucer to practise with, as you can use the indented circle in the centre. Rest the piping tube at the outside edge of the indented circle (or if using a plate, an imaginary circle about 6cm (2½in) in diameter). At the same time, begin steadily squeezing the bag and moving the nozzle around the outside of the circle. Keep squeezing and moving until you get back to where you started,

and continue on the inside of the buttercream circle. You are creating a spiral, which on a flat surface will remain quite flat, but on a domed cupcake will make a wonderful conical shape. Once you reach the centre, release the pressure on the decorating bag and pull it vertically upward to finish the swirl with a soft peak.

Ruffles

Buttercream ruffles are particularly good around the vertical sides of a tall cake, or around the outer edge of the top of a gateau. Choose a tube with a long and narrow opening, either with or without a crimped edge. Practise first on a plate or piece of card. Place the end of the tube at about 45 degrees to the surface, long side down. Squeeze the icing bag and gently but surely move it repeatedly 1cm (½in) back, 5mm (¼in) forwards, to create a ruffled effect.

Dots and lines can be used very effectively to create a wide variety of patterns. Simply picking out the points of a shape with dots can add interest to iced biscuits, as can varying the size of your dots.

Try piping lines radiating out from a central point, either marked or imaginary, for a vintage feel. Play around with different combinations with pen and paper before practising your pattern with icing on card or a plain plate.

When decorating with buttercream, try to keep your hands cool so that it doesn't start to melt in the bag. Keep turning the bag, and put it in the fridge for 15 minutes if it begins to feel too warm and soft.

Knead It!

Nothing compares to the scent of homemade bread baking in the oven. Morning, noon or night, it'll cheer up your home and induce healthy appetites for everyone within its walls.

The most commonly used type of flour for breadmaking is wheat flour. Wheat bread flour has a high gluten content and gives a better volume of bread, as it absorbs more water and makes a lighter dough.

White flour is made from the starchy part of the grain from which the fibre and wheatgerm has been removed. Wholemeal flour is made from 100 percent of the grain; nothing is added and nothing is taken away. Wheatmeal is made from 81–85 per cent of the grain and some of the fibre and wheatgerm have been removed.

Bread can be made with various other grains. Rye gives a dark dough and is usually mixed half and half with wheat flour; barley gives a cake-like texture and is usually mixed with wheat flour; maize gives a crumbly, crunchy texture. Other ingredients can be added to achieve different results: for example, extra bran, wheatgerm, sesame, poppy or sunflower seeds, cheese, herbs, spices, lemon or orange zest and rye flakes.

Kneading

Kneading is an essential part of breadmaking as it helps to develop the gluten and the rise of the dough. Flour a board and use the palms of the hands, almost to the wrists, to push and turn the dough. As you work you can actually feel the texture changing to a smooth, elastic but not sticky consistency.

Don't underestimate the amount of time and energy that's needed to turn your dough from initial mix to perfectly smooth and elastic bread dough. It's a fantastic work out for your arms and breadmaking is particularly good therapy for getting rid of all those frustrations.

Fresh or dried yeast?

Dried or instant yeast can be substituted for fresh yeast.

For 15g (½oz) fresh yeast use 7g (¼ oz) dried or fast-action yeast. For 25g (1oz) fresh yeast use 15g (½oz) dried or fast-action yeast. For 50g (2oz) fresh yeast use 20g (¾oz) dried or fast-action yeast.

- If using fresh or dried yeast, dissolve it in a little warm liquid and leave to go frothy before adding to the other ingredients.
- If using fast-action yeast, add it to the dry ingredients before mixing in the other ingredients.
- If using dried or fast-action yeast, the dough only needs to rise once.

Always check the use-by date on your yeast – dried yeast doesn't keep for as long as you might think and if it's out of date your bread won't rise!

Rising

Always cover the dough when setting it to rise; any draughts may affect the rising process, and even without draughts you don't want the surface of your dough to dry out. The yeast in the dough needs warmth to start working; the ideal temperature is 40–45°C, 98–110°F. Too much heat will kill the yeast; too little will prevent it from working. The time taken for the dough to rise will depend on the surrounding warmth, but it usually takes 1–1½ hours. The second rising is much quicker, usually between 20 minutes and 30 minutes.

Troubleshooting

If the loaf is smaller than expected, the yeast probably did not activate properly due to incorrect temperature during rising. If the texture is coarse, the yeast was not properly mixed at the beginning, or there was too much yeast, which caused excessive rising and air in the dough.

Many freestanding mixers come with a dough hook. This can save you a lot of toil – just follow the manufacturer's instructions for the best results.

Flour Power

The flour we are all familiar with is milled from wheat grains – but it can be made from all kinds of different starchy grains, which is good news for those intolerant to wheat and gluten.

Chestnut flour

Chestnut flour has a natural sweetness and nutty flavour. It works particularly well in dense, chocolatey cakes.

Gram/chickpea flour

Use this sparingly, as it can leave a slightly bitter aftertaste. However, it's great blended with other flours in savoury pastries.

Coconut flour

Coconut flour has a dominant flavour, which works well where you want a coconut flavour, but it's not generally interchangeable with other flours.

Cornflour

Cornflour is great in shortbreads as it lends a 'melt-in-the-mouth' quality. Best used blended with other flours, as it hasn't enough body to be used on its own.

Hazelnut flour

Hazelnut meal flour is available online. Alternatively, you can toast and grind your own nuts.

Linseed/Flaxseed (brown, ground)

The nutty, sweet flavour and high moisture content of this flour makes it a really delicious ingredient. It is often interchangeable with sorghum, millet and gluten-free oat flours.

Millet flour

Allergycare millet flour is available from various online suppliers.

Oats and oat flour

Strictly gluten-free oats and gluten-free oat flour can be difficult to source due to possible contamination from wheat or other cereals in the field or mill – and some coeliacs are sensitive even to pure oats. Millet flour and millet flakes are a good alternative if you'd prefer to avoid oats.

Polenta

For baking, use dry, finely ground cornmeal (not the pre-cooked polenta blocks). It's great mixed with other flours or ground nuts.

Quinoa flour

Quinoa isn't technically a grain, but a seed, and is incredibly nutritious.

Rice flour

Brown rice flour is available online and in some wholefood stores and supermarkets. Glutinous rice flour is also gluten-free: 'glutinous' refers to the stickiness of the rice.

Sorghum flour/juwar

This fabulous flour produces a lovely fluffy cake texture and can be used blended or on its own.

Cassava/tapioca flour

Tapioca flour is similar to cornflour: it's very soft and neutral in flavour.

Best used blended with other flours.

Buying flours

Most of these flours are now available in major supermarkets, although you might have to go to a wholefood shop to find more unusual ones like sorghum or hazelnut flour. They are also readily available online.

Gluten-free baking

Gluten-free cooking can be exciting and creative, and the results utterly delicious. Just like any other cooking, in fact. Some of the ingredients may sound strange at first, but once you get to know them you'll soon get used to them. It's best to focus on what can be done – brilliantly and deliciously – with the resources available. Don't worry about being able to 'translate' traditional recipes to gluten-free precisely, as down this path disappointment and vexation lie.

Gluten-free ingredients

Inspiration from Northern Italy includes polenta, and toasted and ground nuts such as almonds, pistachio nuts and hazelnuts, where these ingredients are commonly used. Ground nuts have a softer texture and higher moisture content than rice flours and typical gluten-free flour mixes. Rice flour is a useful ingredient, but only in combination with other flours.

For cakes that will last longer than just a day or two, the natural oiliness of ground nuts helps keep them moist. Ground linseed/flaxseed is less expensive than many nuts, however, and can be used to replace some or all of the nuts in a recipe.

Linseed has a naturally nutty flavour and a sweetness, and it behaves in much the same way as ground almonds in cooking. Sorghum flour and tapioca flour are soft and absorbent, resulting in light, fluffy cakes. Steer clear of potato-derived flours as they can be heavy, and use gram flour/chickpea flour sparingly as it can have a slightly sour taste. Gluten-free oats and oat flour are great for adding texture, but check that they are certified gluten-free, as this is not always the case.

Tips and techniques

Gluten lends stretch and 'glue' to a batter or dough. In certain cake recipes, the lack of gluten is not so critical. For example, you can achieve a wonderfully textured brownie using ground almonds in place of wheat flour. Pastry, however, is more of a challenge. When making cakes, brownies and other beaten batters, ensure your ingredients are at room temperature and not straight from the fridge. If you add anything too hot or too cold it can cause the batter or dough to shrink during cooking.

If your batter or dough includes beaten eggs, do not pour warm melted butter or chocolate directly onto the eggs, as the heat may cause them to scramble. Baking powder will react with anything acidic and cause the batter or dough to separate, so when adding ingredients to a bowl, try to 'sandwich' the baking powder between other dry ingredients to keep it away from acids such as lemon or orange juice, zest or oil, rhubarb or other acidic fruit.

Pastry

Pastry dough without gluten requires a little TLC. All pastries are easier to handle if chilled in the fridge for an hour or so before rolling out. Use a liberal dusting of tapioca flour and roll pastry between sheets of baking paper. With butter-based pastries and crusts you need to work with chilled and cubed or grated butter.

In warmer weather you'll often end up with a stickier dough and in colder weather you may need to mix it for longer and hand-mould it into something workable. You just need the confidence to manually handle it and swiftly press it into shape. Sometimes you may need to add a little milk or egg yolk as a binder. Pastry is more vulnerable to variables than other forms of baking: room temperature, moisture levels and your body temperature all have an effect. Sometimes the recipe will specify that you bake the pastry blind; this works very well in gluten-free pastry and you don't need to line the pastry with baking beans or baking paper.

Index

National Trust Books would like to thank Kate Shirazi, Emma Goss-Custard and Mike Robinson for the use of recipes from the following books: Baking Magic, Cake Magic, Cookie Magic, Cupcake Magic, Muffin Magic, Honeybuns Gluten-Free Baking and Countrywise Country Cookbook.

Some recipes featured in this book have also appeared in the following books from the National Trust: *Good Old Fashioned Teatime Baking*, *Good Old Fashioned Jams Pickles and Preserves*, and *Tea Classified*.

Picture credits

Photographs on p.20, 27, 32, 40, 42, 44, 47, 48, 51, 52, 57, 59, 62, 64, 67, 68, 71, 79, 80, 82, 84, 86, 88, 91, 92, 174 from Good Old-fashioned Teatime Baking by Tara Fisher.

Photograph on p. 200 from The National Trust Complete Traditional Recipe Book by Tara Fisher.

Photograph on p. 203 from Good Old Fashioned Jams, Preserves and Chutneys by Tara Fisher.

Photographs on p. 180, 182, 185,186, 189 from Honeybuns Gluten-free Baking by Cristian Barnett.

Photograph on page 173 from Countrywise Country Cookbook by Kristin Perers.

Photographs on p. 25, 28, 31, 99, 103, 104, 107, 131, 132, 135, 136, 170 from Cake Magic by Emma Solley.

Photographs on p. 156 and 190 from Baking Magic by Yuki Sugiura and on p. 150 (B) by Charlotte Barton.

Photographs on p. 108, 111, 113, 114, 126, 147, 154, 155, 156, 157, 161, 177, 165, 166 from Muffin Magic by Yuki Sugiura,

Photographs on p. 139, 140, 143, 188, 150, 192, 193, from Cookie Magic by Charlotte Barton.

Photographs on p. 33, 117, 121, 123, 124, 124, 148, 152, 153, 169 from Cup-cake Magic by Charlotte Barton.